Around the Maypole

The Shillingstone Millennium Book

THE MAYPOLE, SHILLINGSTONE.
"A Maypole of exceptional height, carefully guarded with wire stays."

2000

Shillingstone Parish Council

First published in the United Kingdom in 2000
by Shillingstone Parish Council

Edited by Christopher Whitfeld

Cover illustration by
NH publishing

ISBN 1-903583-00-4

GRANT AID

Grants towards the publishing costs of "Around the Maypole" have
been received from:

Millennium Festival Awards for All, Shillingstone Parish Council,
North Dorset District Council, and Dorset Community Action's
Community Project Fund.
We sincerely thank all of them for their help.

Typeset in 10pt Times New Roman

Typesetting and design by Graham Haskell and Paul Hutchins

Printed by Blackmore, Longmead, Shaftesbury, Dorset

CONTENTS

FOREWORDS

What follows is a good story. It's a good story because it's about us – us and all the people like us who have made Shillingstone their home over the past several thousand years and have created the village community of which we are a part today.

To trace the earlier part of our history required research into many sources, while more recent years are still fresh in the minds of our older inhabitants. Reading those parts will no doubt reawaken many a memory.

The future, though, is with the young and it was with them in mind that the Parish Council commissioned this book to celebrate the start of a new millennium – a free copy will be presented to every villager who is 16 years old, or under, on 31st December 2000. Read it, enjoy it and, when the time comes, pass it on to your own children.

Margaret Higgs
Chairman of Shillingstone Parish Council

Little did we know in February 1998 what we had let ourselves in for. Now, over two years later, I know that I write on behalf of all the dedicated producers of this book when I say how much we have enjoyed and learnt from our research, our devilling away to sort out fact from fiction and, in particular, our contact with those people who have opened up their "memory banks" to supply both information and material. The following people were on the Book Committee some or all of the time: Ben Bennett, Mike Dove, Graham Haskell, Margaret and Richard Higgs, June Lisle, the Rev Michael Turner, Isabel and Mike Weiner, Christopher Whitfeld and Bob Yorath.

Starting from the Rev Dr J H Cooke's Shillingstone Parish History, published in 192_, we have travelled far and wide in our research. Sadly, our early and subsequent appeals for more stories and information fell largely on deaf ears. Inevitably, there will be those who will now say: "Why didn't we know?" or: "Why has this not been included?" Nevertheless, we regret that lack of space has meant the omission of some words and pictures.

I thank all the dedicated and long-suffering members for their various contributions to the book. Without doubt the degree of work and time involved has varied immensely, depending on the subject. I feel, though, that I would be lacking in my thanks if I did not pay particular tribute to Ben Bennett, Isabel Weiner and Bob Yorath for the many hours I know they spent on research and writing, to Graham Haskell for his professional advice and guidance on the production of the book and last, but not least, Christopher Whitfeld who accepted the challenge of editing it. My sincere thanks to them all

Mike Weiner
Chairman of Shillingstone Book Committee

ACKNOWLEDGEMENTS

First and foremost, this is Shillingstone's book. It is written by villagers, though of course not without some considerable help from outsiders. It is written, it is hoped, for the enlightenment and perhaps the gentle amusement of present and future generations of villagers. If Shillingstone lasts another 1,000 years, may this book last at least a few.

I add my personal very sincere thanks to the principle researchers and writers – Isabel Weiner, Bob Yorath and Ben Bennett – and to all the villagers who have given freely of their many and varied reminiscences.

Among the younger contributors have been the class three (year six) pupils of 1993 at the village school who have added an invaluable present-day perspective to the school. They are: Year six – Ben Chaffey, Dayna Dowsett, Michael Farrell, Samantha Martin, Nick Mead and Ryan Poole; year five – Emily Udale, Justine Yeatman, Kimberley Martin, Francis Adams, Marc Doble, Mathew Hewitt, Gemma Chalke, Vicky Mathews, Sophie Netherway, Thomas Antell, Cathryn Wright, Oliver Chaffey and Lucy Mothers; and year four – James Abel, Stacey Butten, Hazel Lush, Stuart Brewer, Darren Spiller and Rowena Bowering. Well done to them. They have done a splendid job.

Other writers have been Mike Dove, Richard Higgs, Michael Turner and Sue Rawlinson, whom I also thank along with Mike Morris for his delightful sketches, and Margaret Higgs who typed the bulk of the text. All that this has left for me to do has been to bring everything together and try to ensure reasonable consistency and not too much overlapping and repetition, while attempting to retain individual writing styles which I believe help to give the book some texture and added reader-appeal. On the other side of the editing task, that is to say the printing and publication of the book, I am equally indebted to Graham Haskell and Paul Hutchins at the Blackmore Press. They too have done sterling work and have put up with my nitpicking demands with great forbearance.

Those who have helped the writers have included: Mr Leslie Bailey, Mr and Mrs Percy Butt, Mrs Pam Cole, Mrs Tricia Cooper, Mr Ben Cox, Miss Elyn Crompton, Dr Joan Davies, Comdr Andrew Forbes, Mrs Joan Ford, Mr Robert Fripp, Mrs Hilary Graeser, Mr E Haines, Mr and Mrs Stan Haines, Mr Alan Hammond, Mrs Nellie Hart, Mrs Kitty Jackson, Miss Myra Jones, Mrs D Kelly, Mrs Phyllis Lane, Mrs Brenda Lewis, Mrs June Lisle, Mr Brian Oliver, Mrs Christine Pope, Meriel Lady Salt, Mr Fred Savory, Mrs Margaret Shackell and Dr Geoffrey Tapper.

The researchers' thanks go as well to Dorset County Record Office, Dorset County Archives Service, Dorset County Library, the Local Studies Library in Taunton, Bryanston School Library, Shillingstone CE VA Primary School, Dr P Nockles of the Methodist Church Archives at the John Rylands University Library of Manchester, the Rev Kenneth E Street, Connexional Property Secretary, Central Buildings, Manchester, and members of the Shillingstone Gospel Hall congregation.

Photographs used in Chapter 6, Railway Lines, have been kindly loaned from the J Rimmer, John Sawyer, and Bob Downes collections.

The Tithe Map is reproduced from the 1838 Tithe Map of Shillingstone held by Dorset County Record Office (reference T/SHI).

Christopher Whitfeld
Editor

BIBLIOGRAPHY

Domesday Book, Dorset. Edited by Caroline and Frank Thorn. Phillimore.

The Medieval Foundations of England. G D Sayles. University Paperbacks.

The Black Death. Philip Ziegler.

Royal Commission on Historical Monuments. HMSO 1970.

Listed Buildings Record. North Dorset District Council.

The Buildings of England – Dorset. Newman and Pevsner. Penguin 1972.

Rural Life in Wessex. J H Betten. Moonraker Press 1977.

S & D Memories. Alan Hammond. Millstream Books of Bath 1993.

Stories of the Somerset & Dorset. Alan Hammond. Millstream Books of Bath 1995.

Reminiscences of the Somerset & Dorset. Alan Hammond. Millstream Books of Bath 1997.

Bournemouth to Evercreech Junction. Vic Mitchell and Keith Smith. Middleton Press 1987.

Somerset & Dorset Then & Now. Mac Hawkins. David and Charles 1995.

Methodism in Dorset. John S Simon. C1870.

Methodism in Sturminster Newton. The Rev C A Nurse, Blandford. 1982

History of Shillingstone. Dr J H Cooke.

Captain Swing. E J Hobsbawm and George Rudé. Lawrence and Wishart 1969.

Letters to *The Times* from the Rev Lord Sidney Godolphin Osborne.

Various school textbooks on 19th century British history.

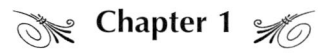 **Chapter 1**

From Earliest Times

"The poetry of history lies in the quasi-miraculous fact that once, on this earth, once on this familiar spot of ground, walked other men and women, as actual as we are today, thinking their own thoughts, swayed by their own passions, but now all gone, one generation vanishing after another, gone as utterly as we ourselves shall shortly be gone, like ghosts at cock crow." G M TREVELYAN

The history of Shillingstone is not that of great events or famous people, but it is rather that of the thousands of men, women and children, throughout many centuries, living out their lives in the same familiar place between the chalk hills and the river, as do we villagers of today.

Before history

We know nothing of the earliest inhabitants of this place but we can assume that it was inhabited at least 6,000 years ago. On the other side of the river, Hambledon Hill is crowned with a long barrow, a Neolithic burial mound dating back before 4000BC, and south along the ridge are the earthworks of a religious enclosure and open cemetery of the same date – Dorset's "Isle of the Dead."

Early peoples preferred to live on higher ground as it was open and more easily farmed. The land where today's village is would have been heavily wooded, and the lower land on three sides very marshy. So the earliest evidence of a settlement is on top of Shillingstone Hill at Bonsley Common where storage pits, some over a metre deep, floored with flint, and containing pottery and animal bones were found last century.

In the Iron Age, from about 500BC the area was inhabited by the Durotridges tribe. Across the valley they built the huge earth ramparts of Hambledon and Hod Hills, each enclosing towns of several thousand population in organised and structured societies. On the flat summit of Shillingstone Hill was a similar settlement, though smaller, protected by the "cross dyke" cutting off the north east spur of the hill. This bank and ditch can still be seen.

There was also an extensive field system, Celtic "lynchets," a network of earth banks dividing small arable fields, which until destroyed by ploughing and forestry about 50 years ago could be seen on the open grassy hillside. The way of life for these early villagers was unchanged for centuries. They lived in small

1

The open grassy hillside above Shillingstone, before forestry and the plough invaded it. This is where the earliest inhabitants of the area would have scratched a living in prehistoric times.

round huts with conical thatched roofs over low turf walls. They were subsistence farmers with a few sheep, cattle, pigs and goats. They tilled their small fields by hand, grew corn and ground it in stone querns, to make flour for a coarse bread. They tended small vegetable plots with onions, garlic and herbs, and gathered wild fruits and nuts. Sometimes they came down to the Stour to fish or trap waterfowl. Their survival was dependent on the weather and the seasons, and so they worshipped the sun and the moon as well as sacred springs, stones and trees – and their ancestors whom they buried in the hilltop mounds, some of which have escaped destruction and are still visible.

They had no need to travel far unless to the meeting and trading places such as Hambledon Hill, but their settlement did lie on an important early trade route, the Wessex Ridgeway which led north to the temples of Stonehenge and Avebury and south to the coast and so beyond to Europe and the Mediterranean.

The Romans

From the Mediterranean in AD43 came the Roman invaders who landed a large army at Poole Harbour, quickly forced their way up the Stour valley and attacked the fortified hilltop towns, including Hambledon and Hod Hills where our early residents may have taken shelter. The defenders' sling shot and spears were no match for the armour, artillery and discipline of the Second Augusta Legion. Blazing beacons on the hills had warned of invasion, but the native settlements were quickly overrun and the area became part of the mighty Roman Empire.

For most of the inhabitants, however, little changed. The village on Shillingstone Hill continued, though now it paid tribute and taxes to Rome, and part of the harvest and produce went to feed the occupying Roman legions. Down in the river valley Roman villas were built. There were sizeable agricultural estates as well as grand houses for the Roman invaders and administrators. The nearest known Roman villas were at Iwerne Minster and near Sturminster Newton, but our local people would have continued to live in their small huts on the hill. Virtually all traces of that Romano-British village have been destroyed by ploughing and cultivation in recent years but the site is marked on large-scale maps and is just discernible. Local coarse pottery together with some finer imported ware has been discovered there. For some years after the invasion a number of cavalry were stationed on Hod Hill and would no doubt have patrolled the area and assisted in the collection of taxes, but apart from the odd Roman coin or shard of pottery we have no evidence of their presence in the parish.

The Roman Empire brought peace and stability; retiring soldiers were encouraged to inter-marry with the local population, and some of the villagers may have been recruited into the army or to work on the network of roads crossing the area or on the villa estates. Some may even have visited the new Roman town of Durnovaria (Dorchester) or travelled as far as Aquae Sulis (Bath), returning to amaze their families with tales of grand stone buildings and hot baths. But for the majority life continued unchanged for almost 400 years. In the earlier years the native Celtic religion would have been supplemented by the Roman pagan gods, and although Christianity was introduced by the 3rd century AD, it is not known whether it penetrated to these remote parts. Similarly the villagers would have continued to speak Celtic rather than the new Latin.

The Saxons

As the Roman Empire disintegrated the legions were withdrawn by AD410 and this part of England was invaded by the Saxons, a warlike tribe from Northern Germany who landed on the South coast and swarmed inland. Initially they came to loot and pillage the defenceless inhabitants. They were opposed by local chieftains such as the semi-legendary King Arthur but they eventually overran much of England. Soon the invasion became immigration and the Saxons brought their families to establish new settlements. The Stour would have been deeper and wider in those days, and they could have brought their shallow-draft boats as far as the hill above the river where Shillingstone's parish church now stands. They chose this site which gave a measure of defence, access to the ford across the river ("oak ford") and surrounding level land which could be cleared for farming. The Saxons used oxen for ploughing and were able to cultivate the rich valley lands, whereas the primitive scratch ploughs used by the Celts were suited only to the lighter soils on the hills.

The new village would probably have comprised a few scattered rectangular one-roomed houses with rough timber walls and thatched roofs, measuring about five metres by three and each occupied by a family for living, eating and sleeping. The house of the chieftain or "thegn" might have been a little larger. An ever-burning fire in the middle of each house was used for heating and cooking and the smoke would have found its way out through the thatch. There would have been other small huts and barns for storage and housing animals and the whole was surrounded by an earthen bank and palisade.

As the buildings were wooden there is rarely any substantial archaeological evidence of Saxon villages, but in Church Field the steep bank at the edge of the level area is probably part of the Saxon earthwork. Aerial photographs indicate that this may have been part of one side of a rectangular enclosure around the higher ground.

The native population with their hill farms were mainly ignored by the newcomers who farmed the ground in the valley, but as the years passed the hilltop village was abandoned and the Celts became assimilated into the Saxon settlement. The landscape around the village gradually changed as trees were felled to clear the large open fields favoured by the Saxons. The furrows were a furlong in length (220 yards) which was the distance the oxen would plough before being rested and turned; the strips were therefore long and narrow, separated by earthen banks. These distinctive "ridge and furrow" patterns can still be identified in some fields to the south and east of the village from aerial photos or on the ground when the sun is low and casts long shadows.

England had reverted to paganism even before the influx of Saxons with their new gods such as Thor and Woden, but Christianity returned to the country with St. Augustine and the heathen Saxons were gradually converted. Tradition is that St. Birinus, the Bishop of Dorchester (in Oxfordshire, not Dorset) came to these parts in AD635 and established the Church of the Holy Rood on its present site. The carved stone head, dug up in the churchyard and reset above the door in the church porch, is said to be of him. The stone grave slab now mounted on the back wall of the church may also be from those early days, as the sun and moon carved either side of the head were pagan symbols taken over by those early Christians. The first church would have been a small timber building and in the past, about 50 feet south west of the tower, gravediggers have uncovered stones which may have been bases for timber or stone pillars and a layer of wood ash which could be the remains of that first church. It would not have had a full-time priest and would have been administered from the Minster church recently established at Sturminster Newton. The dedication of the church to the Holy Rood, meaning Holy Cross, confirms its Saxon foundation.

The village grew and prospered as part of the Kingdom of Wessex, the population increased and more and more land was taken into cultivation. But by AD800 Viking and Danish raiders were swarming into Southern England, though Wessex under King Alfred repelled the attacks better than most. The second Danish invasion in Ethelred's time was more disastrous as Milton and other nearby abbeys were plundered and Danegeld – the Danish protection money – was imposed. By the mid-11th century Anglo-Danish lords owned this part of Dorset.

The Normans

Then in 1066 came another invasion, that of the Normans, who quickly moved across Southern England imposing their rule on the Saxon population, replacing their overlords with Normans and imposing new taxes. The invaders built castles at Shaftesbury and Dorchester to dominate the area and subjugate the population. In 1086 they set about surveying the wealth of the country to ensure that tax income was maximised. This survey, the Domesday Book, provides the first documentary record of Shillingstone.

"Schelin holds Alford (Shillingstone). Earl Harold held it before 1066. It paid tax for 16 hides. Land for 16 ploughs. In lordship 3 ploughs; 5 slaves. 15 villeins (villagers) and 26 bordars (smallholders) with 8 ploughs. A mill which pays 23s 6d; meadow, 200 acres, less 17; pasture 43 furlongs long and 8 furlongs wide; woodland 23 furlongs long and 9 furlongs wide. The value was £16; now £19."

This tells us that there were 46 adult males and, as the survey ignored women and children, we can estimate the total population at around 200. The land held has been estimated at over 7,000 acres comprising meadows, pastures – longer than any other in Dorset – woodland and plough-land, so it was a sizeable manor.

Schelin gave his name to the village at that time, Schelin Okeford, and the same family held the manor for five or six generations when it passed to the Turberville family by marriage. This is assumed to be the same family as Thomas Hardy's Tess of the D'Urbervilles, and the Rector of Holy Rood in 1312 was one John Turberville.

Like their Lord, the villeins held strips of land in the open fields for which they owed labour services – they would work for two or three days a week on Schelin's strips, and do "boon work" at busy times like harvest. A holding of 30 acres or more was not uncommon and, as some of them became wealthier they may have been able to persuade their Lord to "commute" their labour services in exchange for a money rent. Villeins had to pay fees when they inherited their strips, when their daughters were married or when a son wanted to become a priest. On the credit side, they had rights to graze their cattle and sheep on the pasture and common, to a share of the hay from the meadow and to feed their pigs on the waste. They were, however, tied to the land, and could be brought back in chains if they ran away.

Over the next 100 years the population grew significantly and a shortage of farmland led to more woods being felled and land cleared for growing crops. During this period the parish church was rebuilt in stone and flint, and the nave, with its small round-headed windows high in the north and south walls, and the chancel date from the early 12th century.

The manor was subdivided before 1290, when the holding of Bere or Beremarsh was created. The name derives from the old English name given to a low-lying marshy area of scrub and willow. At the rear of Beremarsh farm is an overgrown moated site, probably the site of the manor house. No trace of a building can be seen but the wide ditches still hold water especially in winter. A watermill had been built nearby to harness the waters of the Stour to grind corn. This would have been owned and controlled by the Lord of the Manor, so that he could keep part of the harvest for himself as an additional form of taxation. It was forbidden for any of the villagers even to possess a grinding stone or "quern", to force them to use the mill and pay the tax. The last mill on the site was demolished as recently as the 1920s, and slight remains of the brick building and the mill leat can be seen approximately 200 yards to the east of Beremarsh farm.

Famine and Pestilence

In the early 1300s the climate became much colder and wetter, and poor harvests led to hunger and starvation. And then the village was suddenly hit by the Black Death as it spread across Dorset. It is believed to have been brought into the land by a rat which jumped ship at Weymouth in 1348. This devastating pestilence raged across the land killing up to half of the population. Nobody was spared; landowners, priests, peasants, young and old, rich and poor died agonising deaths and were hurriedly buried in the churchyard. Children and babies who survived the pestilence died of starvation. With nobody to tend them, farm animals died in the fields and yards. The village had no understanding of the cause nor of any treatment to alleviate let alone cure the plague. And then when the village began to recover there was another outbreak in 1361.

So many of the villagers had died, survivors were too few to work the fields, much of which soon became a derelict, weed-infested wasteland. Cottages were

Beremarsh watermill in about 1885 with miller Frank Rickman on right beside the millrace. The mill closed in the 1920s and now only traces of it remain.

abandoned and quickly collapsed and disintegrated. As there were now so few surviving workers, some rent-paying peasants were able to bargain with their lords for higher wages, but the poet Langland tells in "Piers Plowman" that the poorest peasants were "famished with hunger and wretched with the miseries of winter", whilst the landlords "in gluttony glut themselves with wealth."

It was probably at this time that the old village around the church was abandoned and new dwellings were built to the south of the church around a village green, the area enclosed by Church Road and Blandford Road, and a little way down the hill to the south. Cookswell was a separate tiny hamlet. Part of the village was divided into long narrow plots, on each of which a cottage was built. Those bordering Blandford Road, backing onto Hine Town, are typical. The cottages would have been little better than those huts they replaced; flimsy timber frame, walls of cob or wattle-and-daub, thatched roof, hearth still in the middle of the earth floor, no chimney and small windows covered with shutters or rags, glass being far too rare and expensive. The large family lived, ate and slept in the one small room, though there was sometimes a dark, airless gallery or sleeping loft. Many cottagers would have been sharing part of the building with their animals; at least they gave some warmth in winter.

As the population began to recover from the devastation of the Black Death the abandoned fields were worked once again. The farmlands now extended from the village to the hills to the west and to the river to the east, where there were water meadows which were flooded in spring to produce a desperately needed early crop of grass. The hills were extensive open pastures for sheep. Each Friday a market was held around the village cross and each year there were two major fairs held in the village. In 1327 Edward III had approved two yearly fairs. One "on the vigil, feast and morrow of St Barnabas the Apostle." This would have been 10th, 11th and 12th June. The other fair was to be held on the feast of St Dennis. The village green at the Cross was the centre of festivities around the maypole. There was said to be another feast in the form of "a wake held on the Sunday after Holy Rood Day" (14th September). There would have been stalls and pedlars, musicians, and other entertainment. These occasions were eagerly looked forward to as a respite from the unremitting toil in the fields, but for those who cheated or over-indulged there were probably a pillory and a set of stocks set up on the green for the punishment of miscreants, and maybe a village "lock-up".

There was a second preaching cross in the churchyard, from which bread and alms were distributed to the poor. The base of this cross can still be seen by the path, and that of a third cross remained to the south of the village until at least the late 1800s but has now disappeared. From the steps, travelling friars of the Dominican or Franciscan orders would preach. Throughout medieval times the parish church remained the focal point of the village and most would attend services. The religion was of course still Roman Catholic with services in Latin, and the villagers would not have really participated, mass being celebrated behind the rood screen which separated the "public area" of the nave from the sacred area of the chancel and altar. The friars preached in a language that villagers could understand and they were also no doubt a great source of news and gossip about the world beyond the confines of the village, outside which few travelled.

Daily Life

Throughout the 1400s life continued in the village virtually unchanged. Living standards improved little for the peasants but there was evidently sufficient wealth to add the lofty tower to the church to house the bells needed to drive away demons and open a channel to God as well as call the village to prayer. These were days of superstition and the Devil and his works were acknowledged. Illness, poor harvests, natural disasters were all attributed to him and prayer was the only defence, although some villagers may have resorted to the local "conjuror" for magic spells and potions, taking care not to step into the realms of witchcraft.

The inhabitants of the village throughout these centuries would have continued their lives in much the same way. The vast majority would have been tied to the land, toiling from dawn to dusk. Parts of the land surrounding the village were still common land and some villagers would have grazed their scrawny cows on the pasture. The village was self-sufficient but a poor harvest meant hunger, even starvation. Many women, and children as soon as they were old enough, worked in the fields, gathering stones, scaring birds from the crops, and hastening to gather the harvest before the weather changed. Those women not labouring in the fields would work at home, carding and combing wool in the gloom, spinning, scrubbing and mending, and peeling rushlights, the only meagre source of light after dusk. When darkness fell, they laid exhausted on their straw beds, sleep broken by the crying of cold and hungry children. Few villagers would have had any possessions beyond the sparse contents of their mean rented hovels, and certainly no savings to fall back on in hard times.

Several of the villagers would have been tradesmen – blacksmiths, shoemakers, carpenters, wheelwrights, thatchers – with a marginally higher status than the common labourer, but they together with the rest of the villagers were still mostly dependent on the whim of the Lord. These craftsmen were some of the few villagers who would have travelled much beyond the parish boundaries to neighbouring market towns. They walked many miles carrying their wares. A few may have journeyed as far as Dorchester or Salisbury and a few young men may have left the area as seamen or soldiers. Others may have joined monastic orders, perhaps at Sarum, Cerne, Wimborne or Milton. Education for the majority was at best rudimentary, perhaps a few brighter boys being taught to read by the priest in the church porch. The girls and women of the village would have had little reason or opportunity for travel or education.

Religious change

Village life continued oblivious to major upheavals elsewhere such as the Wars of the Roses which ended with the Battle of Bosworth Field in 1485. It was not until the 1530s that national political events would have had any noticeable impact on daily village life. Henry VIII's break from Rome and the dissolution of the monasteries resulted in the closure of the wealthy abbeys at nearby Milton and Sherborne, and the destruction of the massively wealthy nunnery at Shaftesbury. The official religion was no longer Roman Catholicism but Church of England, but the same priest probably continued to officiate, though now in English. The poor had depended on the church and monasteries for some assistance, but the new Poor Laws decreed that they became dependent on the reluctant parish. Beggars, vagabonds and paupers would be whipped and beaten out of the village.

Generally speaking, England was enjoying more wealth and prosperity, a little of which may have trickled down into Shillingstone. In evidence, one of the oldest houses surviving in the village, Greensleeves, dates from the early 16th century and is substantially built around a massive oak frame. The centre part of Long Thatch and part of Cox House also date from the 16th century, albeit the latter part of it.

In 1588 Southern England was threatened by the Spanish Armada and an invasion was expected at any time. Local men would have been recruited into the militia and each night villagers peered into the darkness across the valley to Fontmell Down for the flicker of telltale hilltop beacons warning of the arrival of the Spanish invaders and their dreaded "inquisition." The threat passed and although this was a period of political and religious unrest life in the village carried on as usual.

Over the next 100 years the population continued to increase. In 1539 the muster rolls indicate that there were 53 able-bodied men available for military service which suggests a total population of around 250. By 1642 there were 101 males over 18 years suggesting the population had nearly doubled. And the tide of history reached Shillingstone. The English Civil War between King and Parliament rampaged throughout Southern England, both sides requisitioning men, horses, food, and supplies. Local clergymen and farmers formed a third side, the Clubmen, to try to protect the interests of the country dwellers.

> "If you offer to plunder or take our cattel
> Be assured we will bid you battel."

Greensleeves, dating from the early 16th century, is one of the oldest surviving houses in Shillingstone.

9

On 3rd August 1645 villagers gazed across the valley to see their ragged army of 3,000 local men routed by Cromwell's cavalry on Hambledon Hill. When the parish church was extended in 1888 a row of graves was found, thought to have been those of villagers killed in the skirmish. Leaving only a cannonball, found in Church Field some years ago, Cromwell's armies moved on to achieve victory over the Royalists.

A period of religious intolerance ensued. The jollities and festivities which had alleviated a life of drudgery were banned. The maypole was cut down, the three preaching crosses were destroyed, and the church was desecrated. The original stone altar was smashed as can be seen from the fragment at the base of the tower in the church. At that time the Rector was Richard West who, as the memorial in the north aisle of the church states, "faithfully acted as shepherd with assiduous care and diligence keeping watch over the flock entrusted to him in times uncertain and calamitous."

This upheaval was quickly followed by the Great Plague, and many wealthy families fled from the towns and cities for the relative safety of the countryside. To Shillingstone from London came William Keen who gave the church its fine oak pulpit as a thanksgiving for his survival.

Then in 1685 the South of England was again in turmoil. The Duke of Monmouth had landed an army at Lyme Regis and was marching north to depose King James II, gathering men and support en route. The army was massacred at Sedgemoor and the remnants were rounded up and tried by the infamous Judge Jeffreys. At the Dorchester session of the Bloody Assizes dozens of local men were sentenced to be hanged, drawn and quartered. There are no records to say that the heads of any of the men from Shillingstone were impaled on the railings outside the church in Dorchester, but these events sent a shudder throughout the county and even in recent years naughty children were cowed with threats of "Judge Jeffreys will get you!"

The People of Shillingstone

From 1654 we have the first written history of the lives of the villagers in the form of the parish registers, which give details of baptisms, marriages and burials. May 17th 1654, Thomas Harte, bell carpenter, was buried. Feb 15th 1703, Mary, daughter of Thomas Fletcher, a vagrant or mountebank, was baptised. April 21st 1746, John Porter and Eleanor Rose, aged between them 144 years, were married. For the first time we know the names of villagers, and many of those family names are well known in the area up to the present day. Until this century it is apparent that most girls married boys from within the village and the immediate area and that they spent their whole lives in the village as had countless generations before. The church records also include sworn affidavits that the deceased were all buried in "sheep's wool shrouds" to support the woollen industry. More land was converted to profitable sheep farming, which being less labour-intensive forced down labourers' wages even further. Several new houses were built in the 17th century including part of Cobbles, Gaunts Farmhouse (now Fippenny Cottage), Burlton Cottage, and Beremarsh Cottage (originally a single-storey building). The largest house was the Jacobean Manor House, which replaced an earlier building but which has itself been replaced following a fire in the 1920s.

The end of the 17th century heralded a period of relative peace and prosperity in England. Many of the smaller land holdings had been amalgamated into larger farms, the tenants of which, the yeoman farmers, were becoming relatively wealthy, whilst those who had lost their holdings, often due to the continuing enclosures, became low-paid labourers on the larger farms, without their own animals or produce to supplement their income. There was a polarisation of rich and poor; Squire and Rector at the top, yeoman farmers just below, and the remainder of the villagers at the bottom.

Over the next century several substantial new houses in the village were built of brick and flint by this new class of yeoman farmers, though roofs would still be thatched. Clayton Farm, Hollies, Church House, and Manor Farm House date from this period. Other houses from the same time include Wisteria Cottage, Lilac Cottage, Japonica Cottage, Honeysuckle Cottage, Everett's Cottage, Maypole Cottage, Church Croft and the terraces of thatched houses at the Cross including Calleywell Cottage, No 43 and Cross House, part of which was possibly a barn. An imposing Georgian rectory (now the Old Rectory and Old Rectory Gardens) was built in Church Road. This is believed to be on the site of two 13th century parsonage houses. On the site of the "new" rectory was the large rectory barn. In 1752 the late Rector's wife was accused in court of having virtually dismantled the rectory, disposing of doors, windows, floorboards and even the fireplaces. It was substantially rebuilt in 1890. The common agricultural labourer's family would continue to live in dark, damp, overcrowded cottages with cob walls and leaky roofs, barely surviving on a meagre pittance.

The manor of Shillingstone had passed by marriage from the Turbervilles to the Haseldene family in 1393, and was purchased in 1565 by Thomas Brooksby who in 1567 "became a lunatic by the visitation of God." The manor was granted to Sir Thomas Fresham in 1604 who soon sold it to Sir Edward Coke, the famous judge. The village remained in the ownership of the Coke family until 1759 when it was sold to the Beckfords of Iwerne Stepleton who held it until 1888. Some land was owned by Magdelene College, and an Act of Parliament passed in the 39th year of the reign of Elizabeth I established a charity which funded the building and maintenance of "Hayford" (Hayward) Bridge from the rental of three cottages at Beremarsh (probably now Beremarsh House) and four cottages near "Cuckholds" (Cockswell) Bridge. The records of ownership also give a choice of names for the village: Ockford Shilling, Ockford Skilling, Okeforde Shyllynge, Ockford Eskelling, Ackford Skyllings, Acford Kelling, Shillingaukford, and until recently Shilling Okeford.

The maypole had now been re-erected – from which lads from Okeford Fitzpaine often stole the garlands, jealous that Shillingstone had "the highest maypole in the land" – and there were village fairs and festivals again, including the village wake on the Sunday after Holy Rood Day. The major celebration was May Day, kept on the 9th June which was Oak Apple Day, celebrating the restoration of Charles II plus 11 days lost by the introduction of the new calendar in 1752. Many villagers were no doubt most indignant at the loss of 11 days from their short lifespan. The markets and fairs continued, the celebration of saints' days often marked by "Church Ales" when the churchwardens brewed a special barrel or two of beer for consumption by the village. There were performances by the village mummers, and by visiting players, and the Shillingstone Bull or Ooser (a man dressed in a grotesque mask) terrified the children and imposed itself on every festivity and party.

Tough times

These were the highlights of village life in the 1700s. For most villagers daily life was still a battle. Long, arduous hours were spent following the plough in the freezing winter or sweating to reap the corn before the rains came. A poor harvest still meant hunger, and many families still lived a life of poverty and deprivation as generations had before. Housing was still poor for the majority, with large families in just one damp, dark room. A diet of rough bread, hard cheese and a pottage of vegetables was supplemented by a little bacon fat and the occasional rabbit or pigeon. Poaching was punishable by transportation or worse, but hunger must have driven many to take the risk. The rigours of the Poor Laws had for generations kept the poor in fear of destitution but if illness or disability prevented the labourer from working, he and his family would suffer eviction from their cottage and the degradation of the Poor House.

Drink eased the pain for many. The village was surrounded by acres of cider orchards to produce the working man's drink served on the farms as part of the wages and in the numerous drinking houses. Beer was expensive for everyday consumption, but young men might have been treated to a few pints by the recruiting sergeant and his pressgang seeking to encourage "volunteers" for the huge Army and Navy needed to fight the wars in Europe and North America, and to conquer the Empire. (The Dorset Regiment was the first into India.) Such a life with travel to these exotic places must have seemed a wonderfully attractive escape for many a naïve young Shillingstone lad.

An Act of Parliament passed in Elizabeth I's reign established a charity which funded, from cottage rentals at Beremarsh and Cookswell, the building and maintenance of Hayward Bridge, on the road to Child Okeford.

Hayward Bridge, Shillingstone

It is difficult to envisage how isolated Shillingstone was. Where lorries now thunder through the village was just a track for farm carts, cattle and the occasional pedlar or gypsy. The main route from Sherborne to Blandford followed the high land over Shillingstone Hill bypassing the village and leaving it a rural backwater. Some of the richer inhabitants may have travelled a little further than before. In 1744, the Rector's daughter, Susannah Read, visited London and fell in love. Her father did not approve and one Sunday morning in November, while her family were at church, she walked down to the bottom of the Rectory garden and drowned herself in the murky waters of the Stour. She was 19 years old. Some villagers say her ghost still haunts the river bank. Only a few years later a young bellringer, spurned by a local girl, hanged himself with one of the bell ropes in the church tower.

Towards the end of the century Shillingstone saw more change than for hundreds of years. The completion of the enclosures turned the last villager off the common lands. No longer could he graze his solitary old cow, though he might keep a pig and a few hens at his back door. Smaller farms were consolidated and the few remaining farms in the village expanded and the yeoman farmers used their new wealth to extend or rebuild their houses, to provide more comfort for their families and accommodation for farm servants who "lived in." Several of the redundant farmhouses were divided into tenements, for example Long Thatch, to house in cramped conditions those small farmers and their families who had previously eked out an independent living but who were now farm labourers. At this time towns and cities were growing and the industrial revolution was tempting villagers away. Others left to emigrate to America and the colonies of the expanding British Empire. The needs of the Army and Navy took young men to wars around the world. The population of the village fell significantly and many of the older cottages were abandoned. By 1801 there were only 76 families living in 74 houses, a total of 380 villagers. For those that remained daily life changed little. Most were still involved in agriculture and life was a continuing cycle of backbreaking work in the field even for young children – still picking those countless stones out of the fields. There would have been no education or school until two dames schools were established.

The potato had supplemented the inadequate diet of the working man and his ever-growing family but illness and disease, including smallpox, scarlet fever, cholera and typhoid, and poverty carried off many babies and young children to unmarked graves in the village churchyard. Families slept together in one or two straw beds, keeping their day clothes on and huddling together for warmth. In these conditions disease spread quickly. In 1711 the parish register shows 30 burials, from a population of less than 500, surely an indication of an epidemic. In 1792, of 11 burials five were attributed to smallpox. Those mothers who survived childbirth and drudgery, and those fathers who survived a life of toiling in the fields in all weathers, had no opportunity to save. When they could no longer earn a wage and could not meet the rent on their mean dwellings, mother and father would be parted for ever at the door of the workhouse. Even so, some villagers survived to a ripe old age: Ann Pitman died in 1773 aged 104 and Stephen Bath died in 1742 aged 94.

The Beginning of Change

Toward the end of the 18th century, the village experienced the greatest change for centuries: it was now on the map! The turnpike road from Wincanton and Sherborne through the village to Blandford was opened with toll houses built at Gains Cross (still surviving) and New Cross (demolished). Tollbar Cottages near the Cross suggest another toll gate there. Transport of agricultural produce to the towns and cities was easier and in return the introduction of manufactured goods to the village for the few who could afford them – mass produced pots and pans, clothes, and for those few who could read, books and newspapers. A new canal passing through the parish to connect the Bristol Channel to the Stour at Gains Cross and so to Christchurch harbour was started in 1796, though work was abandoned before it reached Dorset. Travellers now came through the village instead of bypassing it, opening it up to outside influences, politics, non-conformist religion, and news. The Napoleonic invasion scare caused worried villagers to turn their eyes to the hills, scanning the heights for the beacons which would warn of invasion, just as their ancestors had done almost 20 centuries before.

Over those 2000 years great historical events had occurred elsewhere, but for our typical villager in Shillingstone life had changed little throughout the centuries. Long hours of toil on the land, a starvation diet, primitive living conditions, blissful ignorance of the world beyond. From the early 1800s village life would begin to change beyond their recognition, slowly at first but at ever increasing speed throughout the 20th century to the millennium.

Chapter 2

The Victorian Years

On 20th June 1837 William IV died and his niece, Victoria, became Queen of England at the age of 18. Her father had been Edward, Duke of Kent. She married her cousin Albert on 10th February 1840. He was three months younger than she was, and his father was the Duke of Saxe-Saalfeld–Coburg. There were 12 train-bearers, all in white, and the sort of pomp and splendour one would expect on such an occasion.

On 20th December 1837 Henry Stickland and Martha Eyres were married in Shillingstone by the curate, Edward Acton. They were both "of full age." Martha signed the certificate herself; the curate wrote her husband's name and Henry put a cross as his mark beside it. Henry came from Shillingstone and was a labourer; his father, Francis Stickland, was a carter. Martha came from Child Okeford and was a schoolmistress; her father, John Eyres, had been a labourer.

Queen Victoria and Prince Albert had nine children, eight of whom produced grandchildren. Henry and Martha Stickland had two daughters. Sarah Elizabeth was born in 1839 and was buried, aged one, on 15th June 1840. Her sister, Jane, died on 3rd December 1842 when she was only 11 weeks old, of water on the brain. Prince Albert died of typhoid fever in 1861; he was 42 years old. Henry Stickland died in 1847, of tuberculosis; he was 40.

Victoria celebrated her golden jubilee on 20th June 1887 at Buckingham Palace with what she described as "a large family dinner" although she was prepared to admit that the gold plate looked splendid. There were over 50 Royal and Serene Highnesses assembled in her honour. The jubilee was celebrated in Shillingstone with a fête in Cowleaze. There was "a feast of beef and pudding for all the village to which everyone had to bring a plate, knife, spoon and fork, then sports in the afternoon and dancing in the evening."

There is ample evidence of Victoria's accession, her marriage, her children, her husband's death and her jubilees, but how do we know about the Sticklands and about the fête in Shillingstone? We know because since 1st July 1837 copies of entries of births, marriages and deaths have had to be sent to the General Register Office, and the church registers in which baptisms, marriages and burials are recorded have to include particular details. We can discover the occupations of every couple married in the Church of the Holy Rood since 1st July 1837, along with those of their fathers. We know the villages or towns in which they lived at the time of the wedding. We know whether or not they could write their names, whether or not they had been married before and, in most cases, how old they were.

We know something about life in Shillingstone after 1880 because there is a fascinating unpublished memoir of her life written in 1958 by Mrs Portman, whose portrait hangs in the Portman Hall. There are also logbooks, which the master or mistress of the village school had to keep.

It had been laid down in 1812 that there should be three separate registers, specially produced by the king's printers, for baptisms, marriages and burials. The registers for baptisms were to include the names, addresses and descriptions of the parents, and the burial entries were to include the age and abode of the dead person. The Sticklands' marriage is recorded, as are the baptisms and burials of their little daughters, and the burial of Henry. Queen Victoria's grief at Albert's death is fully recorded in her diaries. Martha's grief we have to imagine, as we have to imagine the emotions of all the mourners of the little children and young people whose deaths are recorded in the register of burials throughout the 19th century.

In addition to parish registers, there are national records and the most useful of these are the censuses taken every 10 years from 1801 onwards. The population of these islands had grown enormously during the 18th century and the Government had decided that records should be kept. In 1801 Shillingstone had a population of 380. It had grown to 430 by 1821 but was no more than 503 in 1851 and 546 in 1891. In 1999 the population is just over 1,000. The early censuses were concerned with the number of people in each parish, and with houses, inhabited or unoccupied, and occupations – how many people earned their living from agriculture, how many from handicrafts and so on.

In 1841 the names of people were included for the first time, along with their ages (roughly) and the occupation of the head of each household. Henry and Martha Stickland appear in it, sharing a house with George Hallett, a 23-year-old farm labourer. In 1851 exact ages and birthplaces were given as well as each person's relationship to the head of the household. The 1851 census tells us that Martha, born in Child Okeford, was then still living in Shillingstone. She is described as a "needlewoman" living with her father-in-law, Francis, who was a "pauper agricultural labourer." The parish register tells us that Francis died in February 1855 aged 76 but of Martha there is no more trace – perhaps she returned to her birthplace and might be found in the Child Okeford census or in the burial register at St Nicholas.

Had Henry and Martha rented a cottage from its owner, it might have been possible to identify where they lived in the village. The first detailed map of Shillingstone was drawn in 1838 after the passing of the Tithe Commutation Act. In the Middle Ages land holders had paid one tenth of their income "in kind" to support their parish priest. This tenth, or tithe, which might be paid in corn, hay, pigs, wood, etc, was commuted after 1836 into a money payment, based on the prevailing price of corn and the amount of land held by the parishioner. There had to be a village meeting to agree on the amount of land held, and a map was drawn to show every parcel of land, every path, road and stream, every house, cottage, dwelling and tenement – in fact, every inch of ground in the village and the use to which it was put. The list attached to the map named the holders and occupiers of each parcel of land with its acreage, its use – orchard, garden, arable, etc – and the charge to be paid.

16

Much of the land was owned by outsiders. For example, Henry Ker Seymer of Hanford held almost all of the land between the church and the parish boundary at New Cross, and about 75% of the remaining land within the parish was held by Lord Rivers. Other absentee landlords included the Rev Henry Rushworth Woolley, great-grandfather of the Rev James Crompton who came to this village on his retirement in 1963 and took occasional services in the church before his death in 1967. The Rev Henry, so the story goes, had been intended for the Army but changed his mind when he fell in love with the beautiful Henrietta. After a romantic elopement to Gretna Green the pair were more properly married at St Margaret's, Leicester, and Henry was later ordained. He had a living in the Midlands where he "preached best on port," and left his Shillingstone living to the care of his curate, Edward Acton. His glebe lands were leased to a number of tenants.

There was no dominant landowning family living in Victorian Shillingstone. The largest house was the Manor House, but it seems to have changed hands several times during the past 150 years. It was owned in 1838, and at the time of the 1841 census, by George Thompson Jacobs Esquire, JP. He lived there with his wife Harriet, their small daughter Catherine and four servants – there is a memorial window to the family in the Church of the Holy Rood. Mr Jacobs farmed very little of his land and leased a farmhouse and its outbuildings as well as some arable, pasture and meadow land to William Clayton, who lived – unsurprisingly – at Clayton Farm. Mr Jacobs also owned a number of cottages and tenements, gardens and orchards which were leased to tenants.

The only other "proprietor" who lived in the village in 1841 was the widowed Mary Cox Jnr, described as a farmer, who lived at Cross House and whose two sons, William and James, were tenant farmers. William lived at Lamb House (Hambledon Farm) which he leased with meadows and pastures from Lord Rivers; his brother lived at Cox House and farmed at the opposite end of the parish beyond Gains Cross.

To get some idea of the structure of Shillingstone at the beginning of the Victorian period it is helpful to look at the electoral rolls during the decade after the Reform Act of 1832. In the counties, the ancient qualification for the right to vote – the franchise – had been based on land; all freeholders with property worth at least forty shillings a year could vote. The Reform Act extended the right to those who held copyhold land – an old form of lease – worth at least £10 a year, and to those leaseholders who held land worth £50 a year. This added the wealthier tenant farmers to the numbers of those who could vote for the two MPs who represented each county. In 1840 there were 27 men in the village who had the franchise. As you would expect, George Thompson Jacobs was one of them, as was the Rev Henry Rushworth Woolley – he would also have had the right to vote in his Midland constituency. The curate, Edward Acton, qualified because he occupied a house and land of sufficient value.

Nine of the other electors were tenant farmers. It has been written of tenant farmers that they "rarely do any personal labour whatsoever" – that they "supervised and gave the proverbial pig the proverbial prod while leaning over the proverbial gate." Apart from the Cox brothers and William Clayton there were

Joseph Candy, who lived at what is now Beremarsh Cottages, John Dominy, whose 300 acres were scattered around the village, James Newman of Beremarsh, Jesse Gillingham of White Pit, Allan Lawrence of Church House and John Warren, who lived at Manor Farmhouse. They would all have negotiated leases with the landowners and would have viewed farming as a business from which they could profit.

Mary Cox Jnr, who owned more land than any of the other farmers, could not vote because she was a woman.

A number of the craftsmen in the village were rich enough to qualify. John Johnson, miller, who leased Pear Tree Cottage from farmer John Warren, was also rich enough to employ a living-in servant, Charlotte Hatcher. Two of the seven shoemakers appear on the 1840 roll – James Meaden because he owned his house and garden, and Thomas Gould because he leased Church Croft. Shoemaking must have been a profitable craft because James Dibben qualified for the vote in 1841. Others who could vote were Thomas Sedlen, maltster, who lived at Cobbles with his wife Mary, their seven children and their servant Charlotte Roberts; William Melmoth, carpenter, who lived at Hollies with his wife Elizabeth and their eight children; George Stevens, blacksmith, who lived at The Crooked House with his wife Ann and their five children; Francis Sticklen, butcher, of Long Thatch; and Charles Paine, parish clerk.

Surprisingly, the 1840 list includes Francis Stickland, father of Henry, and the 1841 roll lists William Courage, John Starks and John Gillingham, all described as "labourer" or "agricultural labourer" in the 1841 census. The Tithe Apportionment List shows that quite a number of labourers were freeholders and those who did own their cottage and garden would, at least, have not suffered the crippling poverty which afflicted most of their ilk at that time.

The 1841 census describes 35 men as agricultural labourers and, like farm workers all over England, they would have been very poor. They were hired by the week, or by the day, or to do a particular job, and paid accordingly. Contemporary evidence of their poverty comes from the letters to The Times written by the Rector of Durweston from 1841 to 1875. The Rev Lord Sidney Godolphin Osborne, third son of the first Lord Godolphin, burned with anger at the oppression of agricultural labourers and at their appalling living conditions. In a series of letters to The Times written during the 1840s he railed against the farmers who reckoned that a bushel of wheat, with one shilling added to it, was the accepted wage for a week's work. He pointed out that a bushel of wheat would not feed a large family and that one shilling would not go far in soap, candles, fuel, tea, etc. He saw the question of housing for the poor as being of the utmost importance and it was largely through his efforts that it became an important issue.

There was a system for dealing with poverty in the early 19th century. It had existed since the reign of Queen Elizabeth I, when its growth led to fear of riots and disturbances, and a hatred of begging. As the nursery rhyme warned:

"Hark! Hark! The dogs do bark.
The beggars are coming to town,
Some in rags and some in tags,
And some in velvet gown."

That reflects the fear and hatred town dwellers felt for beggars. Laws were passed making each parish liable for its own poor – paupers were sent home from the new industrial towns to their villages. In the villages overseers were appointed to levy a rate on land, and the money collected was used to find work for the "able bodied" – sometimes in a House of Correction or "workhouse" – and to give relief to those too old, or ill, or young, to work. The system effectively bound the poor to their villages because it was only if they were "settled" that they had a right to be supported by their community.

It also encouraged the payment of low wages. Why pay a generous wage if your farm labourer could count on the parish for help? And it increased the poor rate, for the greater the number of labourers counting on the parish for help, the more had to be paid by those liable. The labourers were demoralised and the farmers were ruined. "Such is the general condition of the labourer," wrote Lord S G Osborne in 1844, "that we are obliged to assist many out of the rates who are in full-time work on full pay: we have to keep all who fall sick with scarce an exception, and to bury all who die at the expense of the ratepayers."

Something had to be done, and the Poor Laws were amended in 1834. Parishes were to form unions to build workhouses. The workhouses, or Union Houses, were to be harsh and strict to discourage people from having to enter them – they were nicknamed Bastilles – there was to be complete segregation of the sexes, tobacco and beer were not to be allowed, and the inmates were to be prevented "from going out or receiving visitors without a written order to that effect from one of the overseers." Shillingstone was part of the Sturminster Newton Union, and a Union House was built to the north of Sturminster on Bath Road, in what is now the refurbished Social Services Centre, Stour View House.

Between 1842 and 1890 Canon Dayman, Rector of Shillingstone, buried nine people who had died in the workhouse. Six of them were over 65 (the only woman among them was 83) but the others were very young – a baby of six weeks died of convulsions, a 2½-year-old died of dropsy, and a four-year-old of tuberculosis. It is recorded in the village school's logbook that several children left to go to the workhouse with their mothers but, equally, there are records of readmissions to the school after a stay in Sturminster – presumably because the children's father or mother had returned to employment in the village.

It can be argued that conditions inside the workhouses, although harsh, were sometimes healthier than in the village tenements. Although families were broken up there was at least some care of the sick in the Union House, and food and shelter for the totally destitute. Living conditions in some of the tenements would still have been revolting to us, with dirt floors, overcrowding, straw for bedding and no sewerage – just a privy at the bottom of the garden. Gardens must have been a great consolation, running as they did from behind the houses to Hine Town or Everetts Lane. They would provide some fruit and vegetables for the family – the Rev Lord Osborne declared that potato food "formed near three-fifths of their diet" – and an escape from the loathsome stench which pervaded many of the tenements and cottages.

The overcrowding is revealed in the census returns. In 1841, in the very first dwelling listed, were two families totalling 17 people – Christopher Courage, farm labourer, his mother Mary, his daughters Eliza, Ann and Caroline, his sons Henry, William, and John, and his nephew James; and Charles Cuff, his wife Jane and their six children. Charles was also a farm labourer and he and Christopher owned the cottage between them. It stood with two other cottages, all with gardens, on the land where Toll Bar Cottages now stand, and was presumably worth less than 40 shillings for each share because neither Christopher Courage nor Charles Cuff had the right to vote.

There were several other labourers who lived with large families. Thomas Percy had seven children, as did William Sticklen, while families of six children were quite common in Victorian times. The children would have helped in the gardens and in the fields at busy times of the year – with planting, haymaking and harvest. Mrs Portman remembered seeing the village boys out bird scaring "with their clappers and shouts of Oy-oy-a-oy-oy." Boys and girls would go gleaning at harvest time; the corn gleaned could be taken to the miller and turned into a bag of flour. A large family had its advantages.

There were large families too at the other end of the social spectrum. Mrs Portman was the sixth of eight children born to Maj Lachlan Forbes and his wife Julia, and she spent her childhood, from the age of three, in what is now Shillingstone House. Her father had soldiered for 15 years in India, serving through the Mutiny of 1857 and, after spending 10 years or so trading with China and Russia in partnership with his brother, he bought land in Shillingstone from

Toll Bar Cottages in the year 2000 – a reminder of the road tolls imposed by the Turnpike Trusts set up to rebuild roads in the 19th century.

20

the Jacobs family and built his house on one of the fields. The family came to live in it in 1880. Mrs Portman was Florence Wyndham Forbes. She had two older brothers whom she scarcely knew, three older sisters and two younger brothers.

She describes a childhood which was fairly spartan with very few toys. She mentions a dapple-grey horse which had lost its legs and had to be pulled about, nailed to a board, and two dolls which she never liked, given to her with strict orders that they were not to be broken. "When such a happy day came" she scattered the sawdust stuffing of one of them on the floor; the other survived for two years but in the end its horsehair stuffing was cut up as trusses of hay for the toy horse. She claims that the children had a starchy diet with very little meat or sugar. She was made to eat hard crusts and told that she would be glad of them "when the Frenchman comes." This was a threat which had been made at the very beginning of the century – "the Frenchman" was Napoleon who died in 1821 – and Mrs Portman marvels at the fact that she was brought up on the legend of Napoleon and yet lived through two wars against the Germans.

Her mother was most particular about cold baths. "Half an inch of water in a flat bath did the three of us and 'pale primrose' scrubbing soap was only used when we were extra dirty." The scrubbing would have been done by a French nursery maid. Octavie Chalet, who appears in the 1881 census, would tell the children how she had fed on rats and mice during the siege of Paris in 1870.

The Forbes children seem to have had no near relations in Dorset but throughout the century there were huge extended families of farm labourers in the village. In 1861 there were 24 Courages, 27 Jacksons and 40 Percys; in 1881 there were 29 Courages, 19 Jacksons and 31 Percys. There were four Courage brothers – William, Christopher, James and George. Christopher's sons George, William and John tightened the family bonds when they married their cousins Lavinia, Tamsey and Harriet, daughters of William senior. Both Lavinia and Harriet went to live with their mother, Mary, at Pepper Hill after the deaths of George and John.

Farming in Shillingstone seems to have followed the Dorset pattern. According to Sir James Caird, who wrote of English agriculture in 1852, its chief characteristics were the breeding of sheep and the consequent enrichment of arable land. The sheep – often as many as 700-800 of them – were driven over the wheat fields to dung them, and folded at night on sown fields which gave them no food. The theory was that the greater the number of sheep there were, the greater would be the quantity of corn. The poor sheep, however, suffered from the constant driving and the crowding and Sir James suggested that it might have been wiser to feed the flocks properly and to enrich the land with guava and bones.

Most of the arable land in Shillingstone was under the hill – Penhill, Hillsfoot, Whitepits down to Enford – while the land between road and river was either meadow or pasture. Mrs Portman remembers hundreds of sheep on the hill, which was bare of trees until comparatively recently, and says that people knew the weather was fine if the sheep went to the top. She would see some of the sheep being shorn by hand in a big barn and cattle yard which belonged to Manor Farmhouse – what she calls the Men's Club (later the Reading Room) was built on the site.

Nearly every man in the village had grazing rights on the hill until William, Lord Portman bought them in. Maj Forbes got a field called Doftlin in exchange for his rights, but his daughter makes no mention of payments to the villagers.

The third quarter of the century is generally known as the golden age of English agriculture. The rising population increased the demand for food; wages were still low; railways carried cattle and foodstuffs easily and quickly to the towns; and there was an increasing use of machinery. An enthusiast for new methods lived not many miles away. The Rector of Sutton Waldron used steam engines for threshing, and made sure that no manure was wasted by keeping most of his stock housed and distributing the manure in liquid form through clay pipes. Whether there were "improvers" in Shillingstone is not known but a close look at the village in 1861 shows that its economy was agrarian. Eleven farmers employed 72 farm labourers, six dairymen and dairymaids, three shepherds and six servants. There were carters, hay dealers, a miller, blacksmiths, gamekeepers and supporting craftsmen like boot and shoe makers, a master mason, two bricklayers, two thatchers and as many as 10 carpenters. There were dressmakers, tailors, milliners and glovers; a butcher, a baker, two shops – which probably sold candlesticks – and two inns, one of which employed an ostler. The village school had 110 children on its register but only one schoolmistress plus a pupil teacher aged 15. The Rector employed a governess, a cook, a parlourmaid and a housemaid. There was also a washerwoman and a turnpike keeper.

Roads had been improved by Turnpike Trusts – groups of local landowners who invested money in rebuilding the roads and who were then allowed to charge tolls for using the improved stretches. There is a former tollhouse near Enford Bottom and there are Toll Bar Cottages next to the village school. There must once have been barriers across the road where the tolls were collected. The gatekeeper in 1851, Frederick Shepherd, is described in the census as over 60 years old and is somewhat of a mystery man. He did not know where he was born and there is no trace of him in the parish registers. He was succeeded by William Cousens who had been born in Child Okeford and who described himself rather more grandly as a "Turnpike Gatekeeper" – most of the gates had pikes (spikes) on them, hence the name.

There would have been different tolls for different road users – wagons, carts, livestock, horse and rider – and the system was not very popular.

 Mrs Portman writes of turnpikes on the way to Blandford and Sturminster, and a charge of 2½d for a two-wheeled carriage. When going to Okeford Fitzpaine they avoided the turnpike in Shillingstone "by driving across the stable field and down the back lane" – presumably Lanchards. She writes that the roads were stoned, not rolled. "The stones were brought to certain places on the road and broken small by men who were regular stone breakers – so many yards for a day's work." But the roads were still so muddy at times that the village women wore pattens to keep their feet clean. Pattens were wooden shoes, like clogs, with iron rings underneath them to raise them out of the mud.

The poorer villagers probably rarely left Shillingstone, though, except to go to local markets and, as a result, most of the marriages in the 1840s and 1850s were local – both bride and groom lived in the village. Those who did come from elsewhere lived no further afield than Child Okeford, Okeford Fitzpaine, Hammoon, Woolland, Stepleton and Melbury. The Stepleton bridegroom was a physician whose father was an Admiral and maybe fought at Trafalgar. His bride was the curate's daughter, Jane Barbara Acton. There is a beautiful memorial in the church to Jane's mother, Eliza, who died in 1817 aged 29. She was modest, prudent and dutiful, and mourned by her ever-loving husband and four little ones. Edward Acton married again and his second wife, Louisa, bore him two more children.

The marriage register shows that there was little social mobility in the village either. Yeomen's sons married yeomen's daughters and, more often than not, the groom was also a yeoman. Craftsmen's sons married craftsmen's daughters – in 1843 Ann Wareham, the daughter of William Wareham, sawyer, married William Shepard, sawyer and the son of a sawyer. The 1861 census shows that Ann and William and their six children – the eldest, Albert, 14 years old, was already working as a sawyer –lived next door to the Wareham family where grandfather John, his son Samuel and his grandson Henry were all sawyers. And all the men recorded in the register when George Moors and Lucy Stone were married were blacksmiths. Perhaps young men were apprenticed and fell in love with the master's daughter, or maybe the idea of a business merger was an attraction.

The memorial in the parish church to Eliza Acton.

At the beginning of the Victorian period as many as 30% of the bridegrooms and brides were illiterate and even in the 1880s, almost 10 years after education had been made compulsory for children aged between five and 13, one in 10 grooms still could not write their name; the same is true of only one bride out of 43. There is also a noticeable change later in the 19th century in the number of brides employed at the time of their marriage. And most of them, apart from a glover, a couple of cooks and seven dressmakers, were servants though very few of them were employed in the village. Canon Dayman's cook and his housemaid came from Devon, and his parlourmaid from Bourton. The Forbes family employed a cook, a parlourmaid, a nurse and a housemaid,

HIC QUIESCIT
QUICQUID MORTALE SIT
ELIZÆ ACTON,
REV. E.H. ACTON A.M. UXORIS, MODESTÆ, PRUDENTIS, PIÆ;
QUAM LUGENT CITIUS ABREPTAM
ET CONJUX AMANTISSIMUS
ET QUATUOR PARVULI;
QUAM AUTEM ÆTERNÆ FELICITATIS,
IPSI MODO DIGNI SINT,
SOCIAM SPERANT SALUTARE.

VIXIT ANN. 29.
DESIIT ESSE MORTALIS 7. NOV. 1817.

as well as a governess and their French nursery nurse, and not one of them was born in Shillingstone. The same is true of the farmers' servants. It seems that the "big girls" left home to go into service elsewhere.

With the coming of the railway in 1863 the catchment area for husbands began to widen, to include places beyond Iwerne Minster, Shroton and Marnhull. Some of the couples met because they were servants in the same big house – James Tom was the gardener at the Rectory where he met Anna Love Spicer and married her – but goodness knows what William Jones, a carpenter from Wensleydale in North Yorkshire, was doing here when he met a girl called Lucy Howe who became his wife in 1880. There was probably much rejoicing in the Rectory when parlourmaid Fanny Darch married dealer William Stickland on 29th June 1853. She was 42. When she died less than two weeks later Canon Dayman implied the sadness they must have felt when he described her as "our family servant, especially dear to us, and very recently married."

Occasional fun, even above stairs, to punctuate the dreary routine and hard work of a servant, is suggested by Mrs Portman's account of a visit to "Prayers" by the kitchen kitten. With the maids kneeling in full view of the family, the kitten was running over their backs while Maj Forbes was leading the entire household in prayer. In one breath he said: "Our Father which art in Heaven, take that damned cat out, hallowed be Thy name." The young Florence Forbes was the only one to laugh as Fallowfield, the governess she loathed, took the kitten by the scruff of its neck and left the room. But there was probably much mirth down in the servants hall later.

The old post office in Shillingstone, opposite the village school.

The Post Office, Shillingstone.

In a letter to The Times in 1849 the Rev Lord Osborne writes of the Dorsetshire poor that "for the most part the ceremony of marriage is not thought of until grounds exist for the preparation of baby linen." A comparison of the marriage registers with the baptism registers suggests that there were not many such weddings – they used to be called "shotgun" – in Shillingstone; there were not many babies baptised within nine months of their parents' marriage.

The registers do show, however, that there were changes in men's occupations during the 60 years of Victoria's reign. During Canon Dayman's first eight years as Rector most of the bridegrooms were farm labourers and their fathers likewise. Among the others was postman Robert Bridle – the penny post was introduced in 1840. It was not until the 1860s that there was a railwayman bridegroom and Canon Dayman never had the chance to officiate at the wedding of an engine driver or a platelayer.

Canon Edward Arthur Dayman was Shillingstone's Rector for almost 50 years. The report in *The Western Gazette* of his death and funeral says of him: "He occupied a high position in the church, of which he was an earnest and consistent minister, and was greatly beloved and esteemed, not only by those amongst whom he resided, but by many friends at a distance." He was born in 1807 at Padstow in Cornwall. He took his BA degree at Oxford in 1830 and his MA the following year. He was ordained priest in 1836 and in 1841 took the degree of Bachelor of Divinity. He was a classicist, a Fellow of Exeter College for 14 years and a tutor for nine years, besides being an examiner in Greek and Latin from 1838 until 1842 when he came to Shillingstone.

He kept the parish registers meticulously, in a beautiful copperplate script, including the date of birth as well as the date of baptism of every child he baptised and, most interestingly, adding the cause of death, in Latin, for almost everyone he buried. His wife Ellen Maria bore him six children, all of them baptised by their father in the parish church. Their eldest son, Edward Arthur, was born on 3rd April 1843 and baptised on 23rd April. A memo, in Latin, in the right hand margin says: "Our eldest son, a most worthy fellow and very much loved, died on 4th April 1864." Edward was buried by the Rev Lord Osborne, but Canon Dayman has added a similar memo in the margin of the burial register, prefaced by the words "Paralysis and paraplegia."

The other Dayman children were Helen Halsey, Walter Wythers, Alice Mary, William Hankford and Francis Stanbury, all born before the end of March 1851. The "young gentlemen" are mentioned in the logbook of the village school when they "kindly showed the children a magic lantern," the women in the family gave most generously of their time to take lessons, especially Miss Alice, and Mrs Dayman who often "desired the children to commemorate her birthday by a holiday." Canon Dayman would have visited the school himself at least three times a week for religious instruction and examination of the children. He was also a trustee of the school.

And he must be credited with the restoration of what the logbooks call "the Maying," when the children were usually given two days' holiday. Hutchins, writing in 1874, tells us that not far from the village cross "stands a lofty May Pole which is re-erected from time to time, and the old customs maintained in full force." The Rev Dr J H Cooke, Rector of Shillingstone from 1903 to 1936, records in his History of Shillingstone that "the great event of the year for Shillingstone from time immemorial was May Day held on 9th June which, under the old style of reckoning, would be 29th May, or 'Oak Apple Day'."

Hutchins gives the full text of an inscription in Latin on the maypole, surely composed by Canon Dayman. The translation which follows must, equally, have been written by him:

THEIR MAYPOLE DECAYED BY AGE
THE RECTOR AND INHABITANTS OF SHILLINGSTONE
KEEPING THEIR YEARLY MAY GAMES
WITH ALL DUE OBSERVANCE
HAVE CAREFULLY RESTORED
ON THE NINTH DAY OF JUNE AD MDCCCL

The fading garland warns how short life's day,
The towering maypole heavenward points the way.
Read thou the lesson – seek to gather now
Undying wreathes to twine a deathless brow.

Dr Cooke describes the day in detail: "Sprigs of oak, with gold tinsel paper stuck on the leaves, were distributed, and the morning was spent in preparing the garlands, flowers being liberally supplied by all who had them. In the meantime a band, usually chartered for the day from a neighbouring parish, perambulated the village, playing at various points.

"The base of the old stone cross, with the maypole alongside, was the rallying point for a mild sort of fair. Booths laden with toys and sweet-stuffs for the small fry, and shooting galleries and coconut shies for the young men and maidens, did a roaring trade.

"Needless to say, the tooting of tin trumpets and the shrill squealing of penny whistles, mingled with the crack of rifles and the shouting of cheap-jacks made a deafening din, in marked contrast to the normal peacefulness of the village.

"Early in the afternoon, nearly the whole population of Shillingstone, and many people from the other two Okefords, and even from Blandford, assembled on the Rectory lawn and danced vigorously for about two hours, then a procession, headed by the Rector in full canonicals, marched to the maypole with beating drums and waving banners, and the garlands having been duly hung amid much cheering of the populace, men, women and children joined hands and, forming an enormous ring or sometimes a double ring, careered wildly round the maypole."

That last sentence evokes the breathlessness and excitement of the dancers – perhaps even Dr Cooke himself did some careering. The maypole had been taken down in 1864 and was re-erected on 14th October 1868. Mrs Portman describes the maypole festival as the great event of the year, with dancing in the morning on the Rectory lawn – she used to dance "The Triumph" with the blacksmith, Tom Stone – more dancing around the maypole in the afternoon, and yet more dancing in the evening "in the great tithe barn which stood where the Rectory stables now are" and where now, in 2000, stands The Coach House where Mr and Mrs Maccoy live. That maypole was blown down in a gale in about 1890 and the festivities were neglected for some years. The tithe barn was demolished by the next Rector, the Rev Charles James Marshall (1891-98), who built new stables in its place.

One of Canon Dayman's most important contributions to the tale of this village was his adding the cause of death in the burial register. He used medical terms and one can only suppose that he conferred with the doctor who signed the death certificate. You might think the causes of death in Canon Dayman's Shillingstone cannot differ greatly from those in our day – people die because they are old, because they have cancer in one of its many forms, have had a serious stroke or have heart disease, or because they suffer a fatal accident. It is true that old age, heart disease and strokes accounted for almost 25% of deaths, but cancer seems only to have claimed 11 victims and only nine deaths were caused by accidents. Many of the others resulted from illnesses which can be treated effectively nowadays.

At the beginning of the 19th century it was beginning to be possible to get protection against one serious infectious disease – smallpox. Edward Jenner, a country doctor from Gloucestershire, who had long realised that dairymaids who caught cowpox rarely caught smallpox, took the pus from a cowpox sore on the

Shillingstone's lofty maypole, restored on 9th June 1850, taken down in 1864, re-erected on 14th October 1868 and blown down in a gale in about 1890.

27

The old Rectory where on May Day "nearly the whole population of Shillingstone... assembled on the lawn and danced vigorously for about two hours."

hand of a dairymaid and inserted it into two cuts he had made on the arm of a boy called James Phipps. After a week James became ill for a day or so but recovered completely. When, soon afterwards, he was inoculated with pus from a smallpox patient, he did not catch the disease. The Latin word for cow is "vacca", and Dr Jenner called the process vaccination. As Governments became more concerned with public health, vaccination was made compulsory for a number of years. The logbooks of Shillingstone school record the visits of Dr Curme to vaccinate children starting in 1876, and Canon Dayman's burial register does not list any smallpox deaths.

Nothing was known about the cause of diseases until 1864 when the French scientist Louis Pasteur proved that they were caused by microbes carried in the air – our milk is now "pasteurised" – and it was not until nearer the end of the century that Robert Koch, a German doctor, identified the microbes, or germs, which caused particular human diseases. It took even longer for doctors and scientists to find how to cure those diseases by giving sufferers what came to be called "vaccines."

One of the most fatal diseases in 19th century England was respiratory tuberculosis. We call it TB; 100 years ago it was called consumption and Canon Dayman used the word "phthysis." It was a major cause of death among the poor, encouraged as it was by poor ventilation and overcrowding. Of the 31 people who died from it in the village, 18 were in their 20s and 30s and a number of them left small children.

In 1906 two French scientists, Calmette and Guerin, discovered a vaccine against the tuberculosis germ. Not available until after World War II, it became known as the BCG vaccine (Bacille Calmette-Guerin) which is still in use today.

Most of Canon Dayman's entries are single words or pairs of words naming the illness from which the person died, such as asthma, "febris" or fever, paralysis (probably a stroke), pneumonia, peritonitis and so on. Medicine has made such gigantic strides during our century that the vast majority of these illnesses can now either be prevented – with vaccines or anti-toxins – or treated; there are antibiotics like penicillin, for instance, new techniques like blood transfusions, and new methods of surgery like transplants. Diabetes can be treated with insulin, and dropsy, or fluid retention, with diuretics.

Some of Canon Dayman's most interesting entries are longer, often written in minuscule script which makes them difficult to decipher. They are sometimes concerned with the personality of the dead person. For instance, he says of Mary Cox Thr that she was an outstanding lady, worn out by old age – she was 89 when she died; of Mary Courage who died of asthma aged 43 that she was "a most worthy lady and a great friend of ours". Ann Warren, who was 86, had had bronchitis for many months and had been "a very special lady."

The other long entries are mostly concerned with accidental deaths. For instance, he wrote of James Courage: "Whilst he was digging chalk between Hambledon and Hod Hills, a sudden landslip almost broke his spine; he died within a few weeks." Christopher Courage fell from a height while haymaking and broke his neck; his former close neighbour, Charles Cuff, was accidentally thrown from a cart and died after a few days. There were deaths caused by fire, or by being dragged under the wheel of a wagon. *The Western Gazette* of 25th November 1870 reports that "as Wombwell's Menagerie was passing through Shillingstone on the way from Blandford to Sturminster one of the men, named James Booth, a drummer in the band, was in the act of getting up on a van when he missed his hold and fell under the wheels. His thigh was broken and his left hand was fearfully lacerated." A week later, the paper reported that "the poor fellow, Booth, died after the amputation of his thigh." Canon Dayman adds that he was formerly a soldier and that he was aged 35.

There were three suicides, the most tragic being that of a 19-year-old Shillingstone girl who was in service with the Creech family in Sturminster. There is a long account in *The Western Gazette* of the inquest into her death on 31st March 1874. "She appears to have taken to heart her mistress asking her about the loss of a pair of trousers, and to have premeditated committing such an act at any time she was in trouble," said the report. She asked for twopenny-worth of rat poison at the grocer's in Sturminster. Mr Thomas Potter told her that it was only sold in threepenny packets and gave one to her, believing that it was for her master. She was found, lying in a cattle-feeder crib – "very poorly", with chattering teeth and "all in a quiver" – by farm worker William Ridout, who took her to the surgery of Mr Leach, the parish medical officer. She told PC Cantle, who helped take her to the surgery, that she had taken poison down by the river. He saw her die at about 10.15 that morning and later found, at the bottom of a ditch, the paper which had contained the poison. Emetics and a stomach pump had been ineffectual – probably because the poison had been quickly absorbed by an empty stomach, according to a local surgeon, James Tarzewell – and a verdict of "suicide whilst in an unsound state of mind" was returned.

What becomes very clear after only a brief look at the register is the high infant mortality. A child who lived beyond the age of two had a good chance of surviving until old age, and a number of those who died "worn out by old age" were over 80.

Lots of babies died within a month of their birth, and the cause of death most often given by Canon Dayman was either "convulsions" or "failure to thrive" – the word he used was "atrophia", or wasting, and it was probably a result of poor diet or hygiene.

There are several sad stories of parents who suffered the death of two babies Amongst them are Josiah and Jane White whose twin sons, Jacob and Esau, died of "wasting" before they were one month old. William Sheppard, sawyer, and his wife Ann lost their first two children – but went on to have another nine. One of the most tragic stories is that of postman Robert Bridle. He and his wife Caroline lost their daughter, Julia Ann, when she was 11 months old. Only seven months later, in 1847, Caroline died of TB aged 24. Robert married again in 1849 and his second wife, Izzett Jane, bore him two daughters, Martha and Sarah Jane, and in 1854 a son, William James, who died of "atrophia", or because he did not thrive, aged seven months. Worse was to follow when Robert himself died of TB in April 1856. Izzett Jane gave birth to a second son just after Robert's death. She named the new baby Robert and one can only imagine her grief when he too wasted away early in June. There is a happy ending to this story though. Izzett Jane remarried just over a year later and had three more children, James George, Love and Sydney. Their father was George Meaden whose first wife had died of TB. He must have wanted to preserve her memory because he and Izzett Jane gave her name, Love, to their daughter.

The village towards the end of the 19th century appears not to have been greatly changed since the early 1800s. The population had not grown much and, despite the proven national decline of English agriculture during the last quarter of the century, Shillingstone still had 37 farm labourers in 1891 to say nothing of another nine people involved in dairy work.

Some of the farmers were descendants of the tenant farmers of 1837. Among them were Walter Cox, John Dominey, Robert Sedlen and Thomas Warren. The Gillingham line was represented by widow Ann Gillingham, aged 77, and the Lawrence line by another widow, Mary Ann. There were three other farmers, Robert Hart, John Sticklen, and Henry Roffey, who had been born in Lambeth but had been farming 120 acres in Shillingstone since the middle of the century.

Chapter 3

Shillingstone at War

1914–1918

The Dorset Regiment was raised in 1702. Besides service in Ireland, the West Indies and many Continental wars, it was the first King's regiment to go to India (in 1754) and it bears the proud motto "Primus in Indus." In 1825 it went to New South Wales to guard the convicts. Through the "Green Linnets," as the regiment was nicknamed, Shillingstone men saw life on every continent. But there are also still in existence muster rolls from the reigns of Henry VIII and Elizabeth I which record the men of the village who possessed arms and were capable of using them.

This ancient spirit still animates the residents of the village, and fortunately there is a full and complete record* of all those who went from Shillingstone at their country's call in 1914 to fight on behalf of freedom and what they believed to be right. During the period before compulsory service Shillingstone, in relation to its population, sent more men in response to the call of the Colours than any other village in Great Britain. It was for this reason that it was decided, by a number of prominent people and *The Times* newspaper, that some recognition should be given to what these men had done – that their patriotism should be adequately rewarded.

The most notable feature of the voluntary recruiting in the parish was that our men began to join up immediately after the declaration of war. Learning from the Rector that 66 men out of a population of 565 had enlisted voluntarily, Mr Basil Thomson (later Sir Basil Thomson) wrote to *The Times* inquiring whether or not this was a record. He also informed Lord Stamfordham, who mentioned it to His Majesty King George V. The letter in *The Times* provoked a friendly newspaper controversy. Other correspondents wrote giving good reports of their villages. These suggested to Lord Northcliffe the idea of starting a Bravest Village Competition, which was entrusted to the Editor of the *Weekly Dispatch*. In order to make it universally known he gave instructions that a circular asking for returns should be sent to the chairman of every parish council in Great Britain. The conditions specified were:

1. That the maximum population should be 3,000;

2. That 31st January 1915 should be the latest date for receiving returns;

3. And that five gentlemen, whose names were given, should be the adjudicators.

Eventually it was announced that the total number of returns was about 400, of which 326 were good enough for analysis. The promised prize was a beautiful cross designed by Sir George Frampton who had patriotically volunteered his services.

* See annex on page 144

There was much wrangling by many parish councils arguing the case for their villages, especially whether they should be deemed villages or hamlets. The Rector of Shillingstone, the Rev J H Cooke, argued the case for Shillingstone most strongly and made three visits to the adjudicators' office in London where he eventually met with success. This, very briefly, is the tale behind the Shillingstone cross which is a memorial to those from the village who died in service to their country.

The War Memorial

The design of the cross for Shillingstone's war memorial was selected by the War Memorial Committee from a book submitted by Messrs Farmer, Brindley & Co Ltd, of London. The choice was that of one of the most ancient and beautiful of Celtic crosses, and the work of copying it was entrusted to this firm. In response to an appeal by the Rector, the Bath and Portland Stone Firm Ltd agreed, from patriotic reasons, to present the Portland stone of which it was constructed. The height of the cross is 12 feet, consisting of two steps, the base and the shaft. The work of the sculptors has been universally admired. On the shaft is the following inscription:

> "This cross was erected by public subscriptions 'in memoriam' of the honourable place taken by this parish in the Great War 1914-1919, and specially of those from its Roll of Honour who gave their lives for their country."

On the base is carved a laurel wreath, within which is the message of commendation, sent by command of King George, which reads: "His Majesty is gratified to learn how splendidly the people of Shillingstone have responded to the call of the Colours. I imagine this must be a record."

24th September 1919 – a memorable day in Shillingstone's history when the war memorial cross was unveiled and the German fieldgun was handed over to the village.

The names of the 25 men who died in that war are engraved on the sides and back of the base:

1914	Edward Philps	1917	Frederick Charles Tooze
	Frederick Newman		William James Laws
	Jack Hart		Reginald Sidney Hart
1915	Walter Inkpen		Frederick Newman
	David Herbert Robins	1918	Albert Edward Adams
1916	John Clarke		Alfred Mesher
	James Light		Sydney White-Rogers
	Jack Stainer		Ernest George Woolridge
	Albert Laws	1919	Arthur John Clarke
	Edward Starks		
	Robert Hart	*Additional Names:*	
	Ernest Inkpen		Percival S Read, 1918
	Arthur Frederick Ridout		Ernest W E Gladstone Read, 1919
	Bertram Inkpen		

An anchor, ancient style, the symbol of hope (Hebrews vi 19), is engraved on the reverse side of the base, and the Latin words "Pro Deo et pro Patria."

A German fieldgun and carriage were awarded by the War Office on the application of the War Memorial Committee through their chairman, the Rector. Sir Basil Thomson did much to further the application, as well as the Earl of Shaftesbury, Lord Lieutenant of the county. Earl Haig also supported the application, referring appreciatively in his letter to the Dorset regiments which served under his command. It is regarded as a good specimen of a camouflaged enemy fieldgun.* The gun-metal plate, presented by Sir Basil, bears the inscription: "Captured in the Final Advance, September 1918. Presented by the War Office to the Parish of Shillingstone in recognition of its magnificent record in Voluntary recruiting."

The original intention was to place the cross in the churchyard and some preparation, in the way of pathways, was made for it, but when it was known definitely that the gun would be awarded to the parish, and when a number of our returning men joined with others in expressing the wish that both memorials should be placed together in a more public place, the subject was reconsidered. The question now arose as to how this could be carried out, and the problem was solved when Mrs Kyrle Chapman offered to give a portion of the allotment field for this purpose. It had been recognised for some time that this corner of the Okeford Fitzpaine road was a difficult and dangerous one, and a grant of £50 from the district council was spent on rectifying this. The consequent widening of the road has been much appreciated. No better or more central position could have been chosen, opposite both the village school and what was then the post office. The preparation of the site was undertaken jointly by the War Memorial Committee and the parish council, the latter contributing £20 from its funds towards the cost of the work.

* *Shillingstone was the smallest village to which such a trophy was awarded.*

24th September 1919 will always be a memorable day in the history of the village, for on that day the cross was unveiled and the gun handed over. The following particulars of this interesting ceremony are taken from *The Western Gazette* of 26th September 1919:

"The Great War, with its miseries, horrors, and tragedies, did not fail to leave its mark upon the village life of Shillingstone. Many returned wounded, or suffering in other ways, from the terrible experiences of modern warfare, and no less than 25 have made the supreme sacrifice. Nevertheless a great deal of satisfaction is derived from the fact that Shillingstone ranked first among all the parishes in England, Scotland, and Wales, by virtue of the large proportion of her men who joined His Majesty's Forces before 31st January 1915, namely 90 men out of a population of 565, a record which will lastingly stand to her credit and to the credit of the men who earned for her such a coveted distinction.

An Open Air Spectacle

"The unveiling ceremony will live long in the memory of those who took part in it. The open space before the memorial was densely crowded and, the weather being fine, the proceedings were most impressive. The clergy and choir robed at the church and were joined at the Rectory by the Bishop of Salisbury (the Rt Rev Dr Ridgeway), and they then proceeded to the site chanting the Litany. There they were met by a procession formed at the station, which, headed by the Blandford Town Band under Bandmaster F Bellows, consisted of a number of ex-Servicemen in uniform or mufti, the Mayor and Corporation of Blandford in their robes, accompanied by the two macebearers, likewise in their official attire, and a number of the parishioners. Seats were reserved for the relations of the men who had died and for the demobilised men.

"The chair was taken by the Rector, and he was supported by General the Earl of Shaftesbury (Lord Lieutenant of the county), the Countess of Shaftesbury, Sir Basil Thomson KCB, Majors Colfox, MP for the division, Dugdale, JP (Fifehead Neville), Seymer; Lady Thomson, Mrs Cooke and Mr E J Cocks (chairman of the parish council), Archdeacon Carpenter, the Revs E R Overton (Vicar of Blandford), who acted as Bishop's Chaplain, M J W Morgan (Rector of Yetminster), B Hill (Rector of Woolland), L S Plowman (Rector of Ibberton), C H Gould (Rector of Hammoon), J Ridley (Rector of Pulham), C S Bower (Rector of Childe Okeford), and F Etheridge (Rector of Okeford Fitzpaine). The following were the members and officials of the Blandford corporation present: The Mayor, Alderman J J Lamperd; Aldermen S J Norman and G Dyke; Councillors B Bance, R Groves, A Cherry, T A Webb, S Pond, G Best, G E Gould and A H Foote, W H Wilson (town clerk), E G Coombes (deputy town clerk), H Shipp (borough treasurer) and G Hunt (borough surveyor).

"In his opening remarks the Rector described the cross and read out the inscription, and also related the circumstances in connection with Lord Northcliffe's competition. He added that they were very much indebted to the sculptors for the way they had carried out their work, and observed that the cross had a double purpose – to commemorate the patriotism of the parish as evidenced in the r record for voluntary recruiting in the first six months of the war, and in memory of those brave men who had given their lives. The majority of those named on the cross died in Northern France and Belgium, but two of them died in Gallipoli, two in Egypt, one in Mesopotamia, one as a prisoner in the hands of the Turks one as a result of the operations in Palestine, one went down in the *Good Hope* off the coast of Chile, and one with the *Queen Mary* in the battle of Jutland.

The Cross Unveiled

"The Countess of Shaftesbury then unveiled the cross, after which the Last Post was sounded by two buglers. The Rector next asked the Earl of Shaftesbury to present the gun, mentioning that it was captured in the final drive, and that none of their men were killed or wounded by it.

The Bishop's Address

"The Bishop of Salisbury, having dedicated the cross, gave an address. He referred to the beautiful appropriateness of the memorial to the purpose for which it stood. Nothing else than a cross could really have put before the people of that place through all time to come the meaning of what that day they had done. It stood to commemorate not merely those who in life offered their service, but those who sealed their service in death.

"The Countess of Shaftesbury then placed a large laurel wreath at the base of the cross and during the proceedings she was presented with a beautiful bouquet of pink carnations and white heather by little Miss Betty Cooke.

Vote of Thanks

"Lord and Lady Shaftesbury, the Bishop, the Mayor and Corporation of Blandford, the Blandford Town Band, who gave their services free, and the representatives of the county and district councils were cordially thanked for their presence, as also were those who by their efforts and gifts had brought the memorial to such a wonderful issue, on the motion of Maj Dugdale, seconded by

No better or more central position could have been chosen for the war memorial – opposite the village school and what was then the post office.

35

Sir Basil Thomson, the vote being carried with cheers.

"The choir, who were accommodated in the school yard, led the singing, the band accompanying. The hymns used were 'All people that on earth do dwell,' 'Fight the good fight' and 'O God, our help in ages past.' The opening prayers were intoned and the responses led by the Rev M J W Morgan, and the service concluded with the singing of the Doxology and the pronouncement of the Benediction by the Bishop.

"There was a public tea afterwards in the schoolroom. A collection was taken in aid of St. Dunstan's Home for the Blind and the War Seal Foundation for totally disabled soldiers and sailors."

1939 – 1945

A few minutes before 11.15am on Sunday 3rd September 1939, families in Shillingstone, along with most of the people of Great Britain, switched on their radios and allowed the old valve sets to warm up prior to Prime Minister Mr Neville Chamberlain's scheduled speech from the Cabinet Room of Number 10 Downing Street, London.

At precisely 11.15am the not unexpected statement came: "This morning the British Ambassador in Berlin handed the German Government a final note stating that unless we heard from them by 11 o'clock that they were prepared at once to withdraw their troops from Poland, a state of war would exist between us. I have to tell you now that no such undertaking has been received, and that consequently this country is at war with Germany."

As the sombre voice of Mr Chamberlain read the prepared statement to the British people, he emphasised his deep disappointment in the culmination of a situation that had its roots as far back as 1919 and a ray of hope for peace in 1938; but for everyone in this country and many other areas of the world, their lives would be changed for ever.

The story of Shillingstone during that traumatic period of 1939-45 is much the same as that nationally although in many respects, due to its rural location, it suffered hardly at all. With the formal declaration of war Shillingstone, as with other Dorset villages, began to implement plans that had been worked out and practised many times during the previous year.

Air raid wardens, first aiders, stretcher bearers and men and women earmarked as "fire watchers" (it was their job to report on the fall and location of incendiary bombs) were designated. A much more ominous and real threat – a possible invasion of this country by German forces – was behind the formation of the Local Defence Volunteers (LDV), whose role would be to hinder and harass the enemy by whatever means they could devise and also give support to regular Army units. With their unique knowledge of the surrounding countryside and hills, they would be a real thorn in the flesh of the German soldier. The initials LDV were humorously purported to stand for "Look, Duck and Vanish", which was a little unfair as each member was expected to lay down his life for his country if necessary.

The blackout was rigorously enforced in the village by wardens who rode around on their cycles to check homes and vehicles. Curtains or light wood frames with blackout material were fitted to windows so that not a chink of light would show outside when the lights were on at night. It was found that a cigarette being lit at night could be seen from 5,000 feet (1,500 metres). Car and tractor headlamps were fitted with metal shrouds with slits that deflected the light down just a few metres in front of the vehicle. Sidelights and rear lights were masked by paper with a subdued light being allowed. Anyone in the village showing a glimmer of light at night was quickly jumped upon by the warden shouting, "Put out that light", or worse! As there were few phones in the village (about 12 at that time), most people who owned them were involved in some way with defence or rescue organisations.

Sturminster Rural District Council bore the responsibility of co-ordinating defensive preparations with local defence committees that were led by parish leaders (or village leaders as they were sometimes called). In Shillingstone this task was undertaken by Mr C R Stride, of Broadclose, his deputy being Mr R Sloper, who owned the garage on the main road at the top of the village.

There was much to consider and organise at this stage of the war and the village defence committee began to draw up and implement contingency plans on the national model with variations to allow for local topographical differences, etc. In the very likely event of invasion and heavy fighting in or around Shillingstone, exercises were held to test the effectiveness of the defence planning, which were overseen by "umpires" wearing white armbands. The umpires duly submitted their reports to the RDC with a copy going to the village leaders and regional defence co-ordinators. This did not always go to plan during the exercises and any failings were quickly and succinctly expressed by those in charge.

Early days in World War II – before the World War I fieldgun was sacrificed, along with the iron railings around the war memorial and the gate, to the military requirements of the new conflict.

One such test was "Breakdown Exercise" held in and around the village from 3rd to 9th August 1942. It was to be assumed that several 250kg bombs had landed near the milk factory and railway station and there were four casualties (two serious and two slight), also the road was blocked by large craters and there was blast damage to the surrounding area. Most of those involved in the exercise had thought that things had gone pretty well, but not so Mr Steptoe of Sturminster RDC. His remarks to the village leader were quite sharp and to the point, which led to the resignation of Mr Stride as village leader. Mr Sloper, as his deputy, took over from that point.

In the main though, the exercises went well and much was learnt from them and proficiency increased until it became almost second nature. There was so much to plan for and lessons were being learned all the time – every eventuality had to be covered. For instance, where to get water if the mains supply was cut? Where were the wells and springs? In fact, there were a number of sites for water; the main ones being at White Pit, Chestnut Farm, the "Stores" near the Reading Room, an orchard in Culverhays Lane, in a garden, Goulds yard and Hillsfoot Farm. Although the river Stour was a most obvious source of water, there were real concerns that it would become heavily polluted during any conflict in the area.

The ARP (Air Raid Precautions) warden and leader of the first aid point were Mr H R Tate and Mrs H R Tate respectively who lived at Church House. Mr Bert White had the job of leader of the fire unit that was situated at the Rectory.

On a more military note, the defence of Shillingstone was given to the local Home Guard commander, Mr R W Brimacombe (who resigned in 1942, his successor being Mr H A Lambert). Good liaison between the Home Guard, Civil Defence and village leaders was of prime importance, but difficult in practice with numerous small sections to control. For instance, the voluntary food warden, Mr J T Sticken, of Cranleigh, Okeford Fitzpaine, had to confer with his deputy, Mr Charles Stone, regarding the issuing of emergency food rations from the Mission Hall. Someone also had to ensure that household refuse was collected, or make provision for its disposal. At one stage it was suggested that the two bomb craters on Chestnut Farm be used as a dumping point, but Mr Steptoe in Sturminster RDC was consulted prior to dumping, in case of objections. It was agreed that wood for fuel could be gathered from Alders Coppice, which belonged to the county council, and from Eastcombe Wood, belonging to the Portman Estate.

Special Constables were briefed. They were Sgt W W Cox and Constables Cardy, Woolridge, Pope and Cox.

Children and their welfare were a top priority, with Mrs Lewis in charge of childcare. With 115 children of various ages to be concerned about, Mrs Lewis and her helpers had no easy task, although the WVS represented by Mrs F W Portman, of Manor House, made sure that help would be on hand when needed.

In war, unfortunately, there is death and this unpalatable fact was not forgotten by the defence committee when, not knowing what sort of hell could be visited on the village inhabitants by the enemy, they made preparations for temporary burials in the field known as Church Close. If the situation was desperate, temporary burials could also take place almost anywhere, provided it was not within 100 metres of a dwelling house, well or spring, and avoiding chalky ground if possible. A temporary mortuary was planned in the stables of Church House and a nearby garage should it be necessary.

The animals were not forgotten as they had their own ARP warden in the figure of Mr R F Pope, of Hillsfoot Farm, although pets were not his main concern – cows were. The milking of cows was a top priority and a census was taken of all parishioners who had this skill. It was revealed that of 27 people listed, 20 were women, three were old men and four were boys; and of these 19 were regular milkers with about 230 cows to milk. At this time (July 1942), there was a village population figure of 446 adults and 115 children, many of whom could be most useful to the war effort.

Even schoolboys were involved in varying ways. Brian Oliver, of Wessex Avenue, who was 13 years old at the time, remembers his job clearly. He said: "Some of us lads were big enough, but not old enough to be enrolled officially as stretcher bearers, although we were stretcher bearers all the same. When I was summoned by a warden I would get on my bicycle and go around the village in complete darkness, to get stretcher teams to report to the first aid post."

It was not all gloom and doom in the blackout. There was the incident in 1940 when, during a routine evening patrol around the churchyard of Holy Rood Church, a warden reached the lychgate area. He saw a dull, white, shimmering light hovering near a grave. His fear of the unknown and his sense of duty fought briefly but he forced himself to go forward towards the strange light, feeling his steel helmet rising as his hair stood on end. As he crept within a few feet of the edge of the grave, a disembodied voice said: "Evening, Bill, nice night". Working on the premise that anyone who knew his name couldn't be an enemy parachutist or a ghost, he looked into the grave and saw the gravedigger with a candle set into a niche and a sheet of galvanised iron propped up against one wall of the grave. It was the candle's reflection from the corrugated iron sheet to the back of the spade that was causing the strange shimmering light. One very relieved warden continued on his way a little later.

The blackout was introduced on 1st September 1939 and mobilisation of the armed forces took place on 3rd September. Following swiftly after that, the first evacuee children were transported from London to safer areas in the rural South. Thousands of boys and girls with bewildered and puzzled expressions left their homes and families for the unknown countryside. Many were crying and holding on to each other as they clutched bags or small cases containing a change of clothes and personal belongings. With a cardboard box containing a gasmask slung around their necks and a large name and address label attached to their clothing, they were shepherded onto waiting coaches or trains for the journey to their new and, hopefully, temporary homes. By 4th December there were already about 4,000 evacuees in Dorset, and Shillingstone was not left out.

Two young sisters, Patricia and Mary McDonald, aged four and five respectively, of Kennington, London, were billeted with Mrs Phyllis Lane at 6 Townsend. With husband Ivor serving in the Army, Mrs Lane was asked if she would look after the evacuees for an unlimited period, for the housekeeping of which she would be paid the princely sum of 8s 6d (42½p) per week each. Rationing had not yet been introduced and food stocks were not yet in short supply although some hoarding had been taking place, so most of the regular foodstuffs were available to provide a reasonable diet. This was to change later but for the moment such tasty meals as rabbit stew or roast beef and Yorkshire pudding were not too hard to come by. So, for the time being, families and evacuees ate reasonably well.

With the 1939 National Service (Armed Forces) Act in full swing and young men being called up, it was left mainly to women, children and older people to fill the gaps left. Schoolgirls and staff in a Dorchester school helped to deliver many hundreds of gasmasks, whilst local children helped to fill sandbags and dig slit trenches. Many young ladies (over 18) were directed to war jobs or they could apply for nursing or the services. Because they came under the Registration of Employment Order, their local exchanges were at liberty to put them where they were required. There was virtually no choice, such was the need of the nation.

There were many groups and organisations throughout Dorset and the country which were beginning to play their part in caring for and supporting families who might need their help in the future. At the forefront of these were the Women's Voluntary Service (WVS) and the Women's Institute (WI).

Asked by the Home Secretary in 1938 to form an organisation to help local authorities, the Dowager Marchioness of Reading began to recruit for the "Women's Voluntary Service for Air Raid Precautions", as it was then called. Lady Reading was appointed chairman and the Queen and Queen Mary, the Queen Mother, became joint patrons.

At the outbreak of war 165,000 volunteers belonged to the WVS, which rapidly expanded to 1,000,000. Their involvement covered everything from finding furniture and clothes for evacuees to running canteens and organising dances to lift the morale of people in the towns and villages. Later, in 1942, there was another brief invasion scare which prompted a sharp increase in training for possible German landings.

One enterprising ex-Army man, a Col Barnes of Maiden Newton, started a Ladies Shooting Class where those who enrolled were taught how to strip and load various weapons, the principles of fieldcraft and how to throw grenades. The idea was to train a number of women for the possible formation of local resistance groups to attack the enemy should they gain a foothold in England. The enterprise was short-lived as the authorities were not at all happy with this "Rambo" approach and it was disbanded by the end of the summer. Of much more importance was the formation of a Housewives Section, a sort of cadet branch of the WVS. There were meetings in each village and WVS speakers gave talks. Those housewives who enrolled were given blue cards to put in their windows which at least made them feel that they were also contributing to the war effort in a small but significant way. They were taught such diverse subjects as "how to tackle incendiary bombs" and "making a batter using dried egg powder and dried milk."

40

You might like to try the batter recipe yourself. You can still get dried egg powder in the supermarkets.

A Wartime Batter Recipe

Ingredients

4 oz (100g) flour
1 tablespoon dried egg
1oz (25g) dried milk

½ to 1 pint (300-450 ml) water
Pinch of salt

Method

Sieve flour, salt, egg powder and milk powder together. Add enough water to make a stiff mixture. Beat well and add the rest of the water. Put to one side for an hour. If you want a richer batter, add an extra egg.

Bon appetit.

By the war's end in 1945 a total of 241 members of the WVS had been killed on duty and the Queen dedicated a roll of honour in Westminster Abbey as a reminder of their dedication to duty in that most traumatic period of our recent history. In 1966 the WVS was further honoured by the addition of "Royal" to its title. Since then the service has been known as the Women's Royal Voluntary Service – a most deserving title and one of which some of the women of Shillingstone can be justifiably proud.

The WRVS is typical of the many organisations, large and small, which came to the fore when needed by the country and a great debt is owed to them all for their dedication and sacrifices during the conflict.

World War II may not have scarred Shillingstone much but there was evidence of a country at war all around. To the ordinary villagers, as indeed in the country as a whole, the first few months of the war seemed an anticlimax as work progressed on defensive preparations. Endless numbers of sandbags were filled, Anderson shelters were built in people's gardens, slit trenches were dug near the school and the parish church. Buckets of sand and water with stirrup pumps were left at strategic points to tackle incendiary bombs and thick sticky tape was put on window panes to reduce the shattering effect should a bomb cause blast damage. There was a vain hope that the war could be confined and stifled on the Continent, but as 1939 gave way to 1940 it was obvious that this would not be the case.

When the German Army marched into Paris on 14th June 1940 France had already decided to surrender and on 21st June the surrender ceremony took place at Compiègne. Now the British people braced themselves for the onslaught to come.

Here in Shillingstone the Home Guard (previously called the LDV) increased their training and activities. By now the members had Army-style uniforms, Lee Enfield rifles and other weaponry. They were taught how to stalk the enemy, lay booby traps and make a variety of horrible anti-personnel devices.

Much of their work involved setting up strategic defensive points around the village and helping out with fire-watching at Sturminster Newton. On top of Shillingstone Hill they manned a tree house which gave them a wonderful view over the village to the north, south and east. The hill was not planted with trees as it is now but was mainly scrub and gorse with the odd tree dotted about. The tree house was near Bonsley Pond and could be reached via the very steep Stickle Path, which was no mean task after a 12-hour shift at work – and carrying military equipment. The big fear at this time was parachutists because it was known that the Germans had formidable parachute and glider-borne forces.

Also about this time Shillingstone lost one of the focal points of its war memorial when the First World War German fieldgun was taken, along with the railings and gate, to help the country's war efforts, as steel was in great demand to make guns, shells, tanks and other military necessities. It was at a public meeting on 18th July 1940 that Gen Headlam proposed, seconded by Mr Browse, that the gun – accepted 21 years earlier as a World War I trophy – should go, along with the railings and gate. The voting was 10 for and one against.

The loss of the German gun to the greater needs of the country was accepted with sadness but Shillingstone was proud to contribute it to the war effort. The school railings stayed because the school was on the main road but any others deemed expendable were removed. Aluminium pots and pans were also valuable items, needed for aircraft components. In fact, anything that could be recycled for the war effort was needed.

Old bones, for example, were desperately needed for a hundred different uses It was little realised by most people that 50,000 tons of bones could make 22,500 tons of bonemeal fertiliser, enough for nearly 100 square miles of land. Alternatively, they could make 3,750 tons of cordite for ammunition. Even the humble chop bone could make enough cordite to fire two cartridges from the guns of a Hurricane or Spitfire fighter aircraft.

Things were happening fast now as Hitler and Goering viewed the English coast through binoculars while laying down the strategy of an aerial assault on the South's ports and coastal installations. Shillingstone Home Guard members increased their patrols and met regularly in the Church Rooms. Rationing had begun and identity cards were issued to everyone. The ration books issued to families entitled each person to the following allowance per week:

Bacon and Ham – 4 oz (100g)	Butter – 2 oz (50g)
Meat – 1s 10d (8p)	Cheese – 1 oz (25g)
Sugar – 8 oz (225g)	Margarine – 4 oz (100g)
Tea – 2 oz (50g)	Cooking fat – 2 oz (50g)

Tinned foods were also rationed on a points system, as was clothing (66 points per year).

There were some items of food "off the ration" that could be purchased if you could find them, such as pork sausages which contained very little meat, pigs' trotters and sheep heads. Luckily rabbits were plentiful in this area and, along with the few chickens mainly kept for eggs, they became one of the staple meats in pies and stews. The ingenuity of the housewife was continually tested as she

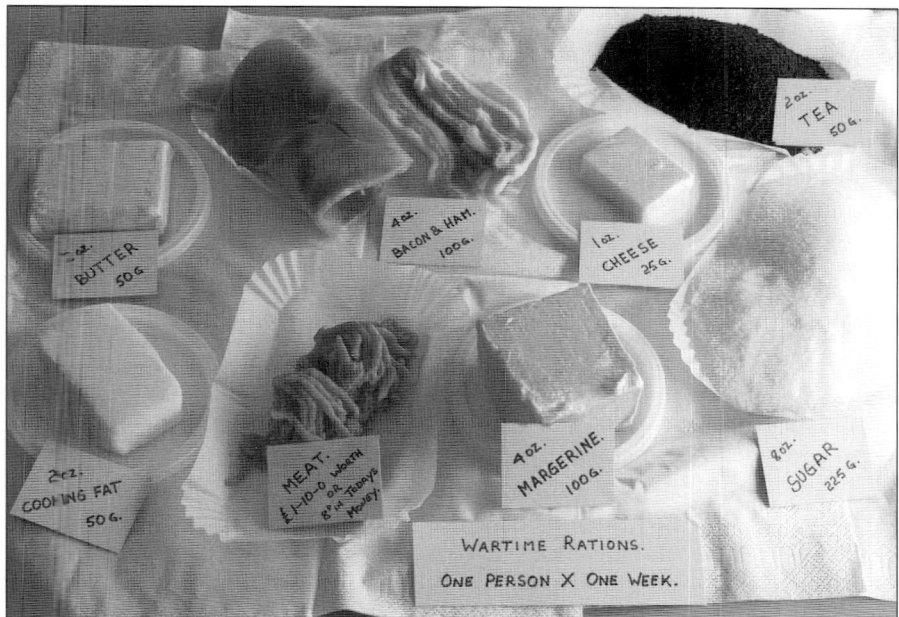

Hard times in World War II – this was the week's food ration for one person.

strove to produce meals that were both nourishing and filling. Households were urged to "Dig for Victory" and to this end flowerbeds were given over to vegetable production. Every spare space that could support a few vegetables did so. Stews were very popular because a little meat could be made to go a long way when used in this way.

Families were often given tips on how to economise and here are just a few. Vinegar instead of eggs: One dessert spoon of vinegar added to ¼ pint (150ml) milk equals two eggs for cake and pudding mixtures. To save coal: Put one handful of common washing soda in a bucket of water and sprinkle over the coal. It makes it burn slower and brighter. Cocoa for children instead of tea: Mix 4oz (100g) cocoa, 4oz (100g) cornflour and 4oz (100g) sugar thoroughly together and keep in an airtight tin for use. Put two teaspoons of the mixture in a cup or mug and pour boiling water onto it, stirring well all the time. Add a little milk if required.

These few ideas were just some of the hundreds offered by the Ministry of Food and other Government departments as a means of reducing imports and conserving stocks of important and essential supplies.

By the summer of 1940 air raids on South coast ports and installations were taking place and as the German Luftwaffe increased its scope of operations to attack coastal airfields the skies above Dorset became a battlefield. Shillingstone was in a fighter control zone and did not have any anti-aircraft guns in the area, although there was a searchlight on a hill near Gains Cross and another at Hammoon.

Typical Wartime Stew Recipe

Ingredients

For stew

1 oxtail	1 large carrot
2 oz (50g) dripping	1 large onion
1 oz (25g) self-raising flour	Parsley. Salt and pepper. Cold water

For dumplings

½lb (225g) self-raising flour	½ teaspoon salt
2oz (50g) shredded suet.	¼ pint water (approx)

Method

For stew

Divide tail into pieces about 1½ inches (37.5 mm) long (cut the thick portion in half lengthways). Wash thoroughly and drain. Heat the dripping and fry the oxtail until it is well browned, then fry the thinly sliced onion. Remove onion, fry the flour until brown then stir in about one pint (450ml) of hot water. Bring to the boil. Return oxtail and onion to the pan; add sliced carrot and seasoning. Simmer for three hours. Add dumplings, cover and cook for a further 25 minutes. Sprinkle a little finely chopped parsley over before serving.

For Dumplings

Sift flour and salt together in a basin. Add shredded suet and mix to a firm dough with cold water. Cut in 16 pieces and roll each lightly into balls. Drop them in boiling water and boil for 25 minutes. They can then be dropped into the stew.

Try this recipe yourselves.

The intensity of the air war over Dorset increased as the Luftwaffe sought targets further inland from the coast and many a Shillingstone lad stood with mouth agape and head tilted back as he witnessed the aerial dual taking place some four miles above. Brian Oliver again takes up the tale:

"If the enemy were heading this way we would be given the air raid warning. Sometimes we could hear Sturminster's siren if the wind was in the right direction, or Blandford's, but we really had to rely on the warden and his whistle. Some of the children who lived close to the school were then allowed to leave for home, the others going to the slit trenches.

"Being boys, we didn't hurry home as there was very often a dogfight going on overhead. We would often see as many as 20 or more enemy planes flying in formation and then our Spitfires and Hurricanes coming down on them from all directions and you could hear the sound of their machine guns as they blazed away. On one occasion a fighter was hit and the pilot baled out – he had been hit in the leg, we heard later. As the plane came spiralling down towards the village, it looked as though it would crash in Shillingstone, but in the last few hundred feet it seemed to level out, eventually crashing at Bere Marsh beside the river.[1] As the ground was quite soft it had buried itself quite deep and it was some time before they realised that the pilot was not in it. However, they did find the officer's peaked cap with a name inked in it and it was later identified as belonging to the pilot who had parachuted to safety. He landed in the area of what is now the Blandford Heights industrial estate.

"Whenever the opportunity arose and we heard of a plane that had been brought down, we would get on our bikes and go and find it, such as at Iwerne Minster where a plane had landed on the side of the hill almost intact – and it was German.[2] I'll bet the crew were pleased to be out of it. There was another at Sturminster Marshall. This one was completely wrecked and I didn't know what it was.[3] Yet another came down at Lydlinch, just behind the new garage on the left as you come from Stur. This one exploded on impact as it must have still had its bombs on board. It was a Heinkel III. I know this is true because I still have a spanner from it to this day. Unfortunately the crew were still on board and it must have been a most unpleasant task for the military to try and gather their remains for burial. Later a machine gun was found hanging in a tree near the Twin Bridges at least 200 yards from the site."

As the summer of 1940 gave way to autumn the air war over Dorset increased in ferocity and aircraft (friend and foe) could be seen trailing smoke and looking for landing places, or crashing mightily in a cloud of smoke and flame. The pattern of the air war also changed at this time as the enemy switched from all-out assault on RAF fighter airfields to bombing towns, cities and other industrial targets further inland.

This new Luftwaffe policy was brought home tragically when, on 30th September 1940, Sherborne was badly hit in a bombing raid intended for the Westland Aircraft works at Yeovil. Bombing through thick cloud, possibly on a beam signal, about 37 Heinkel II bombers unleashed their bombs in a line from Lenthay Common to Sherborne. The bombs devastated much of this lovely Abbey town only a few miles from Shillingstone. In just a few minutes the town suffered 766 damaged buildings, with about 80 completely destroyed, out of a total of about 1,700. Eighteen people were killed and nearly double that number were injured. Incidentally, the 56 Squadron Hurricane brought down at Bere Marsh Farm on 30th September was in action in that raid.

If the schoolboys of the village craved a little excitement, it soon came in the shape of a German twin-engine bomber. On this particular day some of the older boys, aged about 13 or 14, were collecting ashes and clinker in new toilet buckets (flush toilets were a luxury), to put in the bottom of the slit trenches to stop them from becoming a quagmire. They were just about to leave Church House when they heard aero engines in the direction of Hambledon Hill. Being very inquisitive boys, they had to see who could identify the plane first.

---

1 *56 Squadron Hurricane N2434, 30th September 1940.*
2 *A BF110 (S9+DU). Belly-landed beside A350 at The Beeches, near Iwerne Minster.*
3 *Heinkel HEIII (1G+AC) from KG27. Crew of five parachuted safely.*

Initially it was flying towards Sturminster Newton and quite low, it then banked to the left and the boys froze when they saw German crosses on the wings. It came over the railway station and the boys watched in fascination as the bomb doors opened and five bombs tumbled out. The afternoon train had just left the station and it was obviously the target. Not waiting to see the outcome, the boys dropped the buckets and ran at high speed to the school. There was no warning. Even Bill Latham, the warden, who lived next to the garage (now the home of Mr and Mrs Withey) had no time to blow his whistle as the bombs exploded in the field just to the left of the railway line opposite the cricket pavilion. Among the high explosives were a couple of oil bombs that would have vaporised and caused massive blast and fire damage had they worked correctly. Fortunately they did not, although a number of cows were affected by the oil and some had to be destroyed. The pavilion only had some slates blown off the roof and a few shattered. You can see where the new slates are even today.

On the way home from school some of the boys saw a man pushing a bicycle with a misshapen piece of metal on the handlebars which was still warm to the touch. The boys soon found out where the bombs had landed and rushed to the recreation ground to get souvenirs themselves. Most of the rest of the village had also arrived at the scene and a junior officer had a difficult job trying to keep people away from the area. The officer was not too successful as most of the boys managed to collect some souvenirs. Brian Oliver kept part of the tail section of a bomb in his shed until he was married to Dorothy in 1957. He could not remember what eventually happened to his memento.

In late 1940 and throughout 1941 the Luftwaffe again changed tactics and struck at towns and cities throughout the country with most raids being under cover of darkness. The good people of Shillingstone had many a sleepless night as German bombers droned overhead in the late evening or early hours of the morning, en route to attack targets in the West or the Midlands. As the bombers strayed into defended areas the searchlights criss-crossed the sky searching for the invader and anti-aircraft guns put up a box barrage hoping that the enemy aircraft would fly into it. Sometimes they were successful, but mostly not.

The British Government under its new Prime Minster, Winston Churchill, came to the conclusion that the enemy's change of bombing policy was a hint that Hitler was softening up the British people, so the threat of invasion still had to be taken seriously. To this end a hide was constructed in Coombe Wood on Hambledon Hill for the use of British guerrilla forces, the local commander of which was a Maj Wilson. The hide consisted of a nissen hut sunk into the ground and completely covered with earth and vegetation. It had a concrete floor, a 200-gallon water tank, living area and toilet. The observation posts overlooked the Blandford-Shaftesbury road at a point where the traffic would be going slowly to negotiate Stepleton Bends. Fitted with field telephones, it was fully operational in 1941, by which time the secret army ready to man it had been fully trained by No 4 Commando Training Battalion at Poole. Those few local men involved were sworn to secrecy and it was not until the mid 1970s that some details of Britain's secret army emerged.

As the war ground on, food, or the lack of it, was the main preoccupation of most people on "the home front", as it was called. Men, women and children were again encouraged to "Dig for Victory" and many of the remaining lovely gardens were turned over to increased vegetable production to ease the overseas supply situation. Nearly every little patch that could support a few brassicas, onions, carrots or turnips did so.

With many of the men who worked the land in the armed forces, the Government turned to women to help out and once again they did not let the country down.

The Government was well aware that we, as island people, were quite vulnerable to a blockade by German U-boats (submarines), so measures were put in hand before the war to stockpile certain foodstuffs and to take over chief food commodities such as butter, wheat, bacon, cheese – no matter where it was.

At about the same time each county had a War Agricultural Committee that was given powers to increase home food production. Britain was heavily reliant on imported food so it was imperative that a massive increase of vegetables, meat and dairy products was produced; in fact about the only products we were self-sufficient in were potatoes and milk. To help in this respect the Government resurrected an idea from 1917 and the First World War. In May 1939 the call went out for women to join the Women's Land Army and one of the first to do so in Dorset was Mrs Joan Ford BEM (née Bartlett), of 13 Vale Terrace, Shillingstone. In fact she could be the first but as she explained: "Although I was second in the queue behind my friend, who was married, her husband went mad when she told him what she and I had volunteered for. He told her to get her name taken off the list – which she did, so you could say I was number one." This was in July 1939 and straight away Joan Ford was one of the Land Army girls chosen to work on the 600-acre Coombe Farm at Coombe Keynes, near Lulworth Castle. The work was hard and the hours were long on the farm which had mainly cows, sheep, corn and potatoes. For this work Mrs Ford was allowed one week's holiday a year with pay which, if you were over 18, was £3 a week. Out of this had to come her lodgings, which left about half her wages to spend.

The hard work was sprinkled with humour, such as the time when there were War Weapons Week parades in Dorchester and Poole. Joan Ford was driving a tractor on one such parade and on the trailer she was pulling stood a number of Land Army girls holding onto the side chains for balance. Mrs Ford tells what happened next: "Before the parade we were given a short briefing and one instruction was that we had to do an 'eyes left' as we approached the saluting dais. At the appropriate moment the order was given and everyone, including me, did a smart 'eyes left'. Of course, it was not until I had hit the small tank that had stopped in front of me that I realised my eyes should have been to the front, not looking at the dignitaries. Luckily we were only going at walking place so the only damage done was to my pride. I was given a ticking-off though."

Winter was a bad time to be a Land Army girl especially if you were a "townie" and not used to picking ice-covered Brussels sprouts in bitingly cold winds with no gloves.

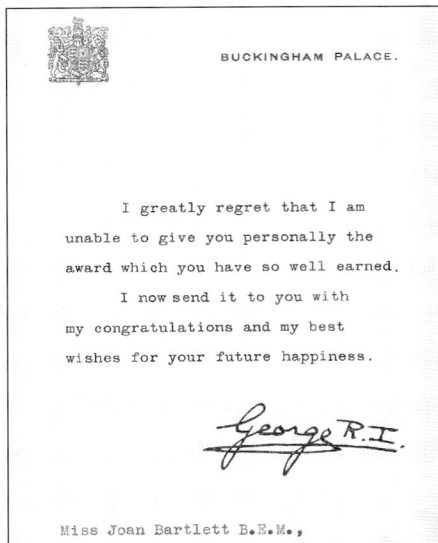

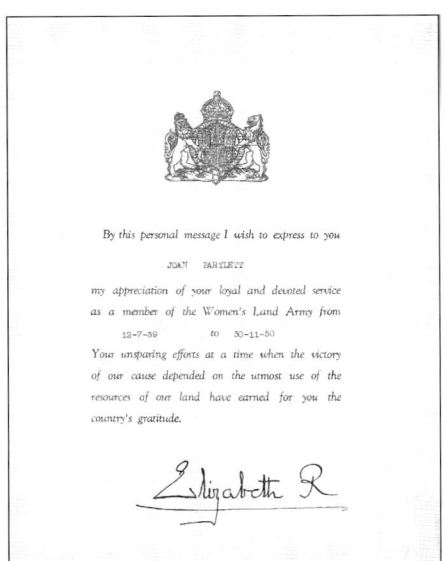

King George VI's letter of congratulations to Miss Joan Bartlett (now Mrs Ford) on the award to her of the British Empire Medal for her services in the Women's Land Army...

BUCKINGHAM PALACE.

I greatly regret that I am
unable to give you personally the
award which you have so well earned.
I now send it to you with
my congratulations and my best
wishes for your future happiness.

George R.I.

Miss Joan Bartlett B.E.M.,

By this personal message I wish to express to you

JOAN BARTLETT

my appreciation of your loyal and devoted service
as a member of the Women's Land Army from

12-7-39 to 30-11-50

Your unsparing efforts at a time when the victory
of our cause depended on the utmost use of the
resources of our land have earned for you the
country's gratitude.

Elizabeth R

... and the personal message of appreciation she received from Queen Elizabeth II when she retired in 1950.

There was no doubt that the Women's Land Army made a significant contribution to helping the hard-pressed farmer to increase the production of foodstuffs and meat for this beleaguered nation during the war and the early post-war years. So impressed was the Government with their efforts that it was thought only correct and proper that an honour should be bestowed on deserving candidates. Thus it was that Mrs Ford was one of only a few members of the WLA to be the recipient of the British Empire Medal, awarded to her on 12th July 1947 by King George VI. She retired from the Land Army in 1950 although she was allowed to keep the uniform.

In late 1943, early 1944, the American Army took over The Grange and other houses from the British Army, which meant that Shillingstone had to get used to another culture and a strange accent. The boys in the village loved every minute of it and the young ladies were also badly smitten by the outgoing and sometimes brash good-looking Americans. As Brian Oliver relates: "I am sure it must have been November because there was snow on the ground and a lot of the Yanks, as we called them, had not seen snow before. It was a golden opportunity for us boys to have snowball fights with them as they had to go past the school on their way to other parts of the village.

"After the Americans had been here a few weeks their officers thought it might be a good idea to invite the villagers for a meal as they had heard that the British were rather aloof so it would be a good way to get to know us. It certainly paid off, because most families at one time or other had one or two GIs to tea on a Sunday. This splendid meal was served up at The Grange (formerly Croft House School and now the Forum School) and was wonderful with everything produced on the same large stainless steel dish. The whole dish was covered with chicken like we had never seen before – it was an American feast. We didn't just get a piece of chicken; it was nearly a whole one each. One of the soldiers said that on the way over on the ship they got so fed up with eating chicken they were throwing them overboard."

Just before D-Day on 6th June 1944 the area, from Lambs Farm to New Cross, was one jumble of boxes and containers as the Americans amassed huge stocks of stores. Almost overnight, it seemed, the stores and most of the American servicemen vanished as the invasion of Europe got under way.

With the departure of the British and American servicemen from Shillingstone and most of the South coast the war on the home front had virtually ended except for the V1 and V2 rocket attacks on London and the Home Counties. The only planes that droned over Shillingstone now were Allied planes going south to support the advance of the Army in the thrust towards Germany.

There were still many shortages in foodstuffs and commodities and rationing was as stringent as ever although the situation was easing slowly. The British people had come through a harrowing experience, with their freedom and that of other countries in peril if they had fallen at the final hurdle. Inspired and uplifted throughout by Winston Churchill's oratory, everyone now waited for the news that Germany had capitulated. Almost 12 months after the Normandy landings Germany surrendered to the Allies at Gen Eisenhower's headquarters at Reims, to be effective on 8th May 1945. After 5½ years of war millions lay dead, permanently disabled or wandering without roots or homes. It would take many years before the situation improved only slightly.

On BBC radio at 3pm on Tuesday 8th May 1945 the Prime Minster announced Victory in Europe Day to the nation, with the following day to be a public holiday. As thousands of servicemen and women, plus anyone else who cared to join in, danced in the streets of London and just about everywhere else, Shillingstone began its own small celebration.

Somehow a group of villagers met up with Reg Sloper and, using his cattle lorry, they carried petrol, diesel oil and paraffin to the top of Okeford Hill and set on fire every shrub and gorse bush they could see. By now the word had got around and other villagers were streaming up Stickle Path to witness and join in the merrymaking. With them, of course, came all of the Home Guard's supply of thunderflashes to help ignite the petrol and make a resounding success of the celebrations. The hill was one wall of fire from the top of Stickle Path to the right of Gains Cross. As was said at the time, "It was comforting to know that it was not caused by enemy action." Other local celebrations included a competition for the best flag-bedecked house in the village. It was not recorded who won.

Despite the joyous occasion, for some Shillingstone families the merriment was tinged with sadness as they remembered their loved ones who went off to war and did not return:

Bertram Ames	Edgar Oliver	Charles Stride
Richard Candy	Douglas Rogers	John Sutcliffe
Bertram Munday	Edward Snook	

On 27th May 1946 a parish meeting was held to discuss a war memorial for the fallen of the 1939-45 war. The chairman suggested the council should defer making any decision but at the parish council meeting of 29th November 1945 it was decided to call another public meeting to discuss the proposed war memorial. The Welcome Home Committee had asked permission for a Portland stone slab with the names of the dead inscribed on it.

Finally, at the public meeting held on 7th December the following resolution was passed:

> "A suitable memorial, in the form of a tablet with the names of the fallen in the last war engraved on it, should be placed in the church, subject to the approval of the church council. Also, a memorial should be placed in front of the existing memorial consisting of Portland stone with the names of the fallen engraved on it."

Mr Bailey stated, on behalf of the Welcome Home Committee, that they would be pleased to help in any way they could with any expenses incurred.

With the war in Europe over, servicemen and women began to drift back home from various parts of the world where they had been serving – to an uncertain future and a changing world. In recognition of their sacrifices and safe return the Shillingstone Welcome Home Committee presented each member of the forces with a brass plaque inscribed:

A few months after the surrender of Hitler's forces in May 1945, the Japanese, after the two atom bombs which destroyed Hiroshima and Nagasaki, also capitulated. VJ (Victory over Japan) Day was a repeat of the VE Day celebrations, although a little less excitable as the Far East war was much more remote and, therefore, did not impact on the lives of this country's citizens in the same way.

Shillingstone, like so many villages, towns and cities throughout the world, had now to adjust to a post-war world. It was not going to be an easy path, but the people of Shillingstone faced it with the same courage, fortitude and humour that they had shown in the blackest days of the war.

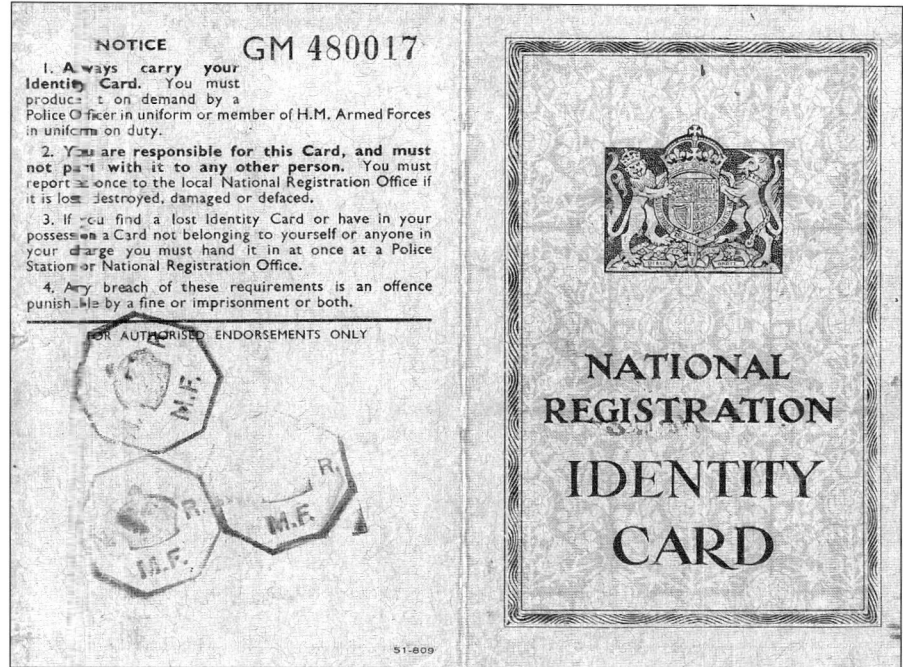

A wartime identity card.

Above: The New Ox, which became The Good Earth tea shop in 1959 and is now Stour House. It was also, at an earlier date, the village undertaker's premises.

Left: Sandy Lane, Shillingstone in the 1920s.

Below: Cottages at White Pit before the fire which destroyed them in the late 1960s.

Sandy Lane, Shillingstone

 **Chapter 4**

Within Living Memory

*At the turn of the millennium some people's memories of
Shillingstone go back a long way, into the late 19th and early 20th
centuries…Other memories are more recent… Some are "about
now"…*

Mrs Julia Forbes, wife of Maj Lachlan Forbes, is fondly remembered for her
contributions in the early years of the 20th century to village school
festivities at Christmas and for giving summer parties in the garden of her Manor
House home, when she would dispense home-made lemonade and buns from the
thatched summerhouse.

It was in the summerhouse that she was seated, deprived of her shoes so that she
could not move – i.e. get in the way – while villagers helped to empty the Manor
House of as many of her possessions as possible to save them from the fire which
totally destroyed it in 1922. Rumour has it that the fire was started in the thatch
when a cigarette was thrown from an attic window by one of the Forbes'
daughters who was smoking up there. But Comdr Andrew Forbes, grandson of
Maj and Mrs Forbes, said an ancient beam had shifted slightly and was too close
to one of the chimneys.

Whatever happened, it was a sad loss of a fascinating house – noted, among other
things, for the fact that it had seven staircases. Within about a year of the fire it
was replaced by the present house.

The property had been bought from the Jacob family in 1879 by Maj Forbes,
along with the land on which Culverhayes (now Shillingstone House and home to
the Salt family) was built. While the Major and his wife lived at Culverhayes,
their daughter Hilda who had married Sir George Lowndes lived for a time in the
Manor House. And as well as her own children Lady Lowndes welcomed into her
home her niece Marigold Portman. Marigold was only two or three years old
when she was sent home from Ceylon by her parents, Lady Lowndes' sister
Florence and Cecil Portman. Not long after this, in about 1913, Mrs Portman was
widowed and thereafter the Manor House became her home on and off, first with
her mother and on her own after her mother's death, until she herself died in 1967.
It was inherited by Comdr Forbes, her nephew, and he and his wife Adelaide
moved in. The Forbes-Lowndes-Portman connection with Shillingstone's Manor
House was finally severed over a century on when Comdr Forbes, by then
widowed, sold it to the Ross family in 1992.

However, the family links with Shillingstone are not totally lost. As well as the
Portman Hall, there is a stained-glass window over the west door in the parish
church which is the joint gift of the Forbes and Lowndes families "to

53

Mrs Julia Forbes – remembered for her Christmas kindnesses and summer parties.

Florence Forbes – who married Cecil Portman, a cousin of the ennobled Portman family of Bryanston.

Marigold Portman – sent home from Ceylon as a child to be cared for in Shillingstone by her Aunt Hilda, Lady Lowndes.

commemorate all the young soldiers and sailors of Shillingstone who lost their lives in the Great War." In particular it is a memorial to 2nd Lt Richard Forbes Lowndes, eldest son of Sir George and Lady Lowndes, who fell in action in 1916 aged 19. And the designers of the window were Florence and Hilda's sister Barbara, who was a very talented artist, and Mary Lowndes who was an aunt of Richard's.

Before the Lowndes, the Manor House had been home for a while to Mrs Kyrle Chapman. Many people in the village remember her as a little woman, always dressed in black clothes – widow's weeds – who sat in the front row in church. Her husband was a churchwarden from 1884 until his death in a hunting accident in 1891, and he helped Canon Dayman to raise money for alterations to the church in 1888. Mrs Chapman became one of the great benefactresses of the village In 1895 she built and furnished the Church Room on land given at a nominal rent by Lord Portman. And in 1902-03 she provided a new roof for the chancel of the church – it is blue with gilt stars – and added a rood screen.

Some say the church now looks naked without the screen – removed in 1977 after a faculty was granted by a consistory court sitting in the church – and some lament the fact that the village cross, restored in her husband's memory by Mrs Chapman in 1903, was later struck by lightning and damaged. Others liked neither her nor her cross. Mr W Dayman wrote to her in May 1893 "basing his objection on the ground of association with the old stones which he thought would be damaged by any restoration" – all that remained of the Saxon village cross in the 1890s was its base, consisting of two steps and a socket. Although Mr Dayman withdrew his opposition a few days later, there was more opposition, this time from Mrs Forbes, and the work was stopped for a few years.

Some village people remember how Mrs Chapman demanded deference. She "expected to be doffed to, and for the young women to be curtseying." There is a story that one day while out walking she met the young Samuel Laws, a member of her scripture class, who greeted her with a "Good morning, Ma'am." "Where is your obeisance to me, Samuel?" she asked. When he merely gaped at her in reply,

Shillingstone's Manor House in about 1910...

55

she became a bit more explicit. "Your bow, Samuel!" "Oh," said he, "I left it at home."

In 1904 Mrs Chapman built Shillingstone Grange – later part of Croft House School and now home to the Forum School – where she lived until she died in 1938 aged 91. Mrs Hilary Graeser's grandfather, Mr James Burgoyne, had been the gardener at the Manor House and expected to go to the Grange with the rest of the servants when Mrs Chapman moved. They were very disappointed when their mistress said: "New house, new servants," and sacked them all.

Mr Percy Butt was given his first job in the garden there when he left school in 1928. He is convinced he got the job because he went to church regularly and was a bellringer. "She was a very religious lady who hosted silent retreats for parsons," he said. She had a chapel at the Grange and some of the stained glass from its windows has now been set in the west window of the parish church's north aisle – commemorating Croft House School's links with the church.

Mrs Chapman employed six gardeners, at a weekly cost of £5, as well as a butler, a cook, a lady's maid, a parlour maid, two housemaids and a kitchen maid. Some of her staff lived across the road in what were called Grange Cottages. (One of these was demolished in 1999 to make way for a terrace of three new low-cost homes, and the other two are now one house, Stukely.) During the winter a weekly box of vegetables was sent up to Mrs Chapman's London house, with flowers

Percy and Doris Butt were jointly awarded Shillingstone's Baldock cup in the first year of the new century, for their services to the village over much of the last century. The cup has been awarded annually since 1978 – the first recipient was Janet Burton – for a variety of services to the community. (This picture was first published in the Blackmore Vale Magazine.)

from the greenhouse for her Chelsea church, and Mr Butt remembers the abundance of flowers she sent every week to the village church.

She is remembered by Mr Butt's wife Doris (née Eaton) as a speaker on Empire Day and as the provider of the school Christmas tree and the presents which came with it. Her coachman, Mr Stone, would drive up to the school from the Grange, sounding his horn, and then play Father Christmas. Later, when the tree was stripped of its decorations, the children would be given the glass baubles from it.

Although she owned a car – first a Wolseley and then a Rolls Royce – Mrs Chapman preferred to travel by coach. Mr Stone wore a top hat with a cockade, and the garden boys had to brush the drive at the Grange to obliterate the wheel tracks when a journey was over.

Mrs Chapman would give a summer party in her garden for the Sunday School children but the food was dispensed by her staff and she would appear only very briefly. She continued to attend the celebration of Empire Day, and these celebrations became more and more elaborate over the years. In 1926 Mrs Forder, who lived in Shillingstone House, gave an address to the children on the West Indies and her husband presented each child with an Empire Medal. There were two addresses the following year. By 1929 the proceedings started with prayers for the Empire followed by patriotic songs, a lecture on Australia, the singing of the National Anthem, and a march past the flag. By 1930 the flag was being saluted.

SHILLINGSTONE gentry in the 1920s also included Mr and Mrs Amherst Webber who lived at Croft House, built originally by Canon Dayman for his daughters, it is said. Mrs Nellie Hart (née Inkpen) remembers Mr Webber's mother as an Italian woman who wore a white lace cap and smoked a clay pipe. Her son was a composer. His arrangement of "Now once again our hearts we raise,' for two choirs of sopranos, altos, tenors and basses, is printed as an appendix to Dr Cooke's Shillingstone Parish History, as is the music he wrote for Dr Cooke's Burial Hymn. It seems likely therefore that he enlarged Croft House by building the music room.

Mrs Webber organised Whit Monday tennis tournaments on her grass courts and provided handsome prizes. Mr Leslie Bailey won the mixed doubles one year and was presented with a canteen of cutlery which he still uses today. She would also invite the village choirs to sing in the music room at Croft. The male-voice and ladies' choirs both competed in the annual choral festival at Weymouth. Mrs Hart was envious at the age of 17, a year too young for membership, as she watched her mother go off to Weymouth wearing a beautiful blouse with leg-of-mutton sleeves.

Mrs Hart was, however, a member of the church choir and took part in some of the annual sacred concerts which began in 1925. In that choir too were Denis Pope, Leslie Bailey, two Coles boys and three Fudges. Visiting soloists came from the London Choir School, for instance, from the Chapel Royal, from Hampton Court and from Winchester Cathedral – but Shillingstone was well represented by Mr G F Coles (baritone) and Bertram Munday (treble). Mr Alexander Popham, who lived in Manor Farm House, was the organist and it was probably he who enlisted support from outside the village. At the 1928 concert, for instance, the organ was played by Mr Sydney Nicholson, sometime Master of the Westminster Abbey Choristers. Mr Bailey, who hoped desperately, but in vain, that a tenor voice would replace his treble, was taken by Mr Popham to Kent for a concert. On the way they stopped in London so that the 12- year-old boy could try his voice in Westminster Abbey and St Paul's Cathedral while Mr Popham played the organs there.

On Armistice Day there was often a Three Okefords concert in the Village Hut – provided for Shillingstone by Mrs Webber and remembered with enormous affection by many people as a place where they had great fun, "far more than in the Portman Hall," say its supporters. There was a ping-pong club for the older teenagers, ballroom dancing lessons were given by Miss Agnes Williams, wonderful "socials" were enlivened by dancing to records played by Mr Marsh from Sturminster Newton, and whist drives were awesome and off-putting to beginners like Mrs Christine Pope who once suffered a grilling when she trumped her partner's ace.

Mrs Webber's chauffeur, Mr Newman, penned some verses to "The Lady of the Croft" which show how well she was regarded by all who knew her. They ended with the lines:

> "Yes, for the cause of truth and right
> She lives and works with all her might.
> And when her earthly course is run
> She'll hear in heaven the words 'Well done.'"

Mr ROBERT Fripp remembers when Mr and Mrs Harry Tate lived in Church House it was filled with "bits of Empire." There was a marvellous sitting-room decorated with spears, shields, lots of dark, exotic wood, and an elephant's foot umbrella stand. Mrs Tate was "in charge of sundry good works and was very much the presence in the village." She befriended Mrs Fripp and suggested that the young Robert, a member of the church choir, should audition for a choir school. Thanks to her, he was launched into an education which took him from Salisbury choir school to Canford School and on to Bristol University.

Mr Tate was chairman of the Three Okefords Horticultural Society and Mrs Webber, Mrs Forder, Mrs Chapman and Mrs Portman head the list of vice-presidents and donors of prizes in the schedule for the show in 1938. Mrs Portman presented a prize for the best "Nosegay of Wild Flowers" picked and arranged by a child attending school in the area. Her prizes of 2s 6d, 1s 6d and 1s were doubled if the flowers were named. One of Mrs Chapman's prizes was for the best cultivated plot in the school garden. And for those children who wanted something to do during the long summer days, there were prizes presented by the Three Okefords British Legion for the largest and best collection of white butterflies – the crops in the gardens must have benefited as well as the prizewinners.

What else could children do for pleasure in an era without television and computer games? For the young Leslie Bailey a really good day out might be spent at Gains Cross watching cars returning from the Wincanton races. When he was only seven, and already mad about cars, his father had once allowed him to drive their Austin 7 home from school and he kept in practice on his father's land near what is now Keeper's Cottage. When he was a little older he joined the thriving tennis club at the recreation ground and remembers the courts being almost always full.

Christine Pope played hopscotch on the main road. She also bowled an iron hoop, made by Mr Blandford the blacksmith at his forge just two doors down from where she lived at the bakery, down the road – there was very little traffic then and most of it was horsedrawn. Some years there would be a craze for spinning tops. There were paperchases on the hill, games of Fox and Hounds, and warm summer days spent floating on bundles of rushes in the river.

For younger children there was a lot of fun to be had in the recreation ground, playing football, rounders or shinty – a game like hockey introduced in 1936 by Miss Harvey when she was the village schoolmistress. It was fun too sliding down Shillingstone Hill on hessian sacks or trays.

Mrs KITTY Jackson (née Ricketts) missed being close to the "rec" and the hill when she returned with her family to live at Toll Bar when she was 13 – she had been born there but spent most of her childhood at Townsend. There was only one year to go, however, before she left school in 1937 and went into service at Child Okeford Manor, and farmer Cox let the Ricketts children play in his field.

Mrs Jackson returned to Shillingstone when she joined Mrs Webber's household in 1938. She did some housework and waiting at table, and enjoyed her work even though her day started at 7am. She moved with Mrs Webber to Little Hanford in 1939 and stayed there throughout the war – Mrs Webber's "war work" was to turn her house into a maternity home which had two nurses and Mrs Jackson's best memory was when she was allowed in on a birth.

The 1930s were difficult times. In 1933 one in four of the working population was unemployed and the situation did not begin to improve until 1939 when war broke out and conscription was introduced.

Mr Butt saw families walking through the village with all their possessions packed around the baby in the pram. They walked to the labour exchange in Blandford in the hope of getting a job there, on to Shaftesbury, and then to Sturminster Newton where the circle began again. Mrs Pope's father, Mr Bartlett, would give bread to those who came into his bakery asking about jobs – at a time when his price of 4d for a 2lb cottage loaf was being undercut by the Co-op bakery in Child Okeford – and the head gardener at the Grange would sometimes hire extra men at the labour exchange.

Mrs Irenee Haines' mother was widowed in 1933 and her pension of a guinea a week – just over £1 – included allowances for her three children. To make ends meet she worked at the Rectory, at Church House for Mrs Tate and at Shillingstone House for Lady Chesterfield. She also knitted gloves. The materials were provided and the gloves were collected by a Mr Blandford. Mrs Bastable earned 9d or 10d a pair – less than 5p. Small wonder that she was aghast not long before she died in April 1999 that her daughter had spent more than 50p on a birthday card.

THE Bastable family lived in one of three cottages which have been made into what is now Calleywell Cottage. There was one room downstairs with a lean-to kitchen where there was running cold water. The bedroom upstairs was shared by Mrs Bastable and her daughter while the two Bastable boys shared the attic. The only lavatory was at the end of the garden. The front door gave directly onto the street, with two steps down to the pavement. There was a fire in the downstairs room with an open grate and a side oven. In that oven Mrs Bastable cooked all manner of good things. There were bread puddings – she never wasted anything – milk puddings, and baked suet puddings.

Mr and Mrs Hart and her husband – not related to Mrs Nellie Hart – lived in one of the other two cottages. Granny Hart "took in washing" in those days before the advent of laundrettes and electric washing machines when people who had no servants could afford the services of a washerwoman. Mrs Haines remembers the steamy kitchen where Granny Hart soaped the linen on a scrubbing board, boiled, rinsed, starched and ironed it before entrusting it to her to take it back to its owners. Mrs Sloper from the garage across the road was one of them, and there were the elderly couple who lived in a thatched cottage next to Greensleeves who used to give her a penny for herself which she had to put in a money box when she got home.

WHILE many of the children leaving the village school found jobs in the village, some went to the nearby towns. Mrs Doris Butt was apprenticed as a dressmaker at Cherrys in Blandford where she earned 4s 6d a week. The most hectic tasks for her were the altering and fitting of mourning clothes. There was always a good stock of them but it was a rush to alter them to fit in the short time before a funeral, and families liked to go into black as soon after a death as possible. A school friend of Mrs Butt's went to Hicks in Sturminster Newton where she earned only 2s 6d a week, and Mrs Pope earned the same princely sum when she began work at Cherrys as a hairdresser. There was not much left after they had paid their train fares from the village into town.

SOON after the death of King George V in January 1936 Shillingstone was saddened by the death of its Rector, Dr Cooke. He had ministered in the village since 1903 and had comforted bereaved families during the 1914-18 war. He was a frequent visitor at the school – he was chairman of the managers – and gave generous prizes to those who did well in his scripture examinations, whether or not they were members of his church. In his black straw boater he would attend Empire Day celebrations and prizegivings. The children picked snowdrops to put on his grave, and the books from his library were set out on school desks and sold to the general public.

Dr Cocke organised, and probably paid for, choir outings in open-topped charabancs to places as far afield as Wookey Hole, and Bembridge on the Isle of Wight, and he would provide afternoon tea on the way home.

THE story of how "Lugeon" Robins got his nickname is told by Meriel, Lady Salt. As a young farm worker he was sent up to the garage to buy some "solution." So as not to forget it he kept repeating the word to himself and by the time he reached the garage he knew it off by heart – he wanted some "lugeon." They all burst out laughing and he had to show them what he had been sent for. The name stuck and nobody ever did know what he was really called.

Lugeon was, as many people know, famed for the cider he brewed in a wooden shed at his home. Anyone who called was welcome to sample the golden liquor – "out of two rather chipped enamel mugs which he cleaned with a bit of sacking," said Lady Salt.

He worked for Mr Michael Pitt-Rivers at the Larmer Tree Grounds at Tollard Royal and another tale about him relates to the collection of 19th century archaeologist Gen Augustus Pitt-Rivers. "Lugeon was asked to stay on one day after the public had left the grounds," said Lady Salt. "They wanted him to dig a grave to bury one of the old mummies because it was beginning to fall to pieces and the mice had been nibbling at it." When he started digging, people kept driving by and interrupting him for a chat. Eventually the job was done but his next worry was that he ought to say a few prayers, and what should he say? Divine inspiration must have come to his aid, and so, as Lady Salt put it, "that was how Lugeon buried his mummy."

TRADITIONALLY across the country, housing for the less well-to-do was provided in the form of "tied cottages," where residency was dependent on the tenant being employed by the cottage's owner. As late as 1950 a family was evicted from a farm cottage at Gains Cross – Mr Butt, a worker-tenant, had taken an unauthorised half day off to visit his wife and newborn child in hospital.

Times were changing however. The programme of council house building in Shillingstone, started before World War II, gathered pace as first Vale Cottages were built on the east side of Blandford Road and then Wessex Avenue, Pepper Hill and Coombe Road rapidly swallowed up the area of allotment gardens on the west side, followed by the addition of Schelin Way in the late 1980s. Initially eight houses in Vale Cottages were reserved for ex-servicemen. Agricultural workers might qualify for subsidised rent. And a village policeman was to occupy the single new house next to the Townsend development, though that "tied" arrangement ended in the 70s and the house went onto the private market.

In the 1980s and 90s Government incentives to sell off council homes led to most of those in Shillingstone being bought by their occupants, resulting in a huge improvement to the look and character of them. Housing associations took over responsibility for the rest, as well as for meeting further needs – examples of their newer homes are to be found at White Pit and Knapps.

At the entrance to Vale Cottages is the archway-cum-bus shelter which marks Shillingstone's commemoration of Queen Elizabeth II's silver jubilee in 1977.

The old parish almshouses (Parish House) opposite Gaunts Farmhouse, available at a low rental (2s 6d a week) to the old and needy, had for long been a cause of concern. They were cold and damp and in need of much renovation – in 1944 the parish council had declared No 1 to be unsuitable for children – but six more years were to pass before the Ministry of Health approved a demolition order. In the meantime, building work on the Eventide Homes went ahead, to become known as Vale Terrace.

On the private housing front, the 1960s and 70s saw the developments at Stour Close and Honeysuckle Gardens, followed in the 80s by Spencer Gardens and in the 90s, after the closure of Croft House School, by Oak Court in part of the Croft garden. The village, backed by North Dorset District Council, has resisted other speculative development in such areas as Hine Town Lane and Church Field.

THERE were a number of recurrent themes for local debate throughout the latter half of the 20th century, one of them being a new road to bypass the centre of the village. This topic first cropped up in 1952 when Sturminster Newton Rural District Council advised the parish council that the proposed route would conflict with the suggested site for a new school near the recreation ground. The bypass debate continued, with some preferring a southern route, some the old railway line and others rejecting a bypass altogether until, in 1998, a parish meeting asked that the proposal for a Shillingstone bypass be removed altogether from the county structure plan. But there could be more to come in the future on this contentious issue.

And what of the very name of the village? Should it be Shillingstone, Shilling

Ivor Lane was in the team that built the previous footbridge some 40 years earlier.

Okeford or even Shillingstone Okeford? This provided another subject for warm discussion.

Public rights of way in and around Shillingstone found a worthy champion during the second half of the 20th century in Mrs Ruth Colyer who was always ready to do battle with individuals and authorities alike to ensure that paths were not lost but rather upgraded and maintained. For many years, too, Shillingstone rights of way officer Mr Stan Haines walked the village footpaths to ensure they remained clear and negotiable. It was in tribute to him and his counterpart in Child Okeford that in 1998 a new footbridge over the Stour connecting the two villages was named the Wilson-Haines bridge.

OLD Shillingstone families have lost some of their cohesion as younger generations have moved away in search of jobs and more affordable housing, while newcomers have arrived from all quarters, in many cases to fill the newly built private housing. The changing population meant fresh blood and new interests to stimulate the old.

Among the most notable of those "incomers" who have for varying lengths of time made their home in Shillingstone over the past half century have been a nationally acclaimed craftsman in wood and silver, Cecil Colyer, television

The new Wilson-Haines footbridge over the Stour was officially opened on Saturday 26th September 1998 – and named after Child Okeford's and Shillingstone's long-serving footpaths officers.

broadcaster and writer Jack Hargreaves, and journalist Christopher Booker's parents John and Peggy Booker.

By contrast, there have been and still are some much longer threads of continuity. Doreen Sloper served as parish clerk for over 40 years, earning an MBE in the 1994 New Year Honours list for her loyal efforts, while Ivor Lane was an active parish councillor for a similar period, and chairman for many years. Both of them also served on the village school's governing body and helped to keep the Methodist Chapel up and running. Roy Paulley has lovingly tended the cricket square, and the recreation ground in general, for many a year. Mike Dove, having been master of ceremonies at the opening dance in the Portman Hall, was chairing its management committee over 40 years later. Jean Churchill was a leader of the Brownies for 34 years. Sylvia Stokes continues to serve the parish church, in the choir and as sacristan, as she has done for more than 50 years...

By the labours of such people, and by the mixture of old and new, do village communities continue to thrive.

Shillingstone's parish councillors in 1994, with their honoured clerk, celebrating the centenary of town and parish councils. Back row from left: Mr Richard Angell, Mrs Helen Lamper, Mr Mike Dove, Mrs Margaret Higgs, Mr Steve Burton. Front row: Mrs Ruth Colyer, Mr Alan Long, Lt-Col Mike Weiner (Chairman), Mrs Doreen Sloper MBE (Clerk), Mrs Sylvia Churchill.

The Shillingstone Song

The Shillingstone Song was composed in 1973 to celebrate the 50th anniversary of the Women's Institute in the village. It recaptures something of the flavour of the village at the time it was written. It goes to the tune of "Among My Souvenirs," and is best heard sung by its author Fred Savory...

Shillingstone we like you, with ample things to do,
There's a sports field too, the recreation ground.
Some views they are serene, the air is pure and clean,
Conditions never been as good as they are now.
Les Bailey with his lime, Fred Light with church clock time,
Nobby Power to keep in line with all the laws of drinking.
Charlie Miller's dairy good – to drink his milk one should.
For a walk there's Bonsley Wood before you go to bed.

Phone kiosk painted red, Jim Farmiloe for your veg,
A haulier man named Reg to move you to your home.
The cricket club so good, hen houses made of wood
Where the S & D once stood, to take you into town.
Two bakers men have we – Latcham and Savory –
And builders we have three; there's also two antique shops.
Street lighting's a dead loss, a post office run by Ross.
Mr Plumpton, he's the boss of Shillingstone Primary School.

We have a football club, a Hall and Woodhouse pub,
Arthur Woodley's shop for grub and meetings at the hall.
If tennis is your game, Mrs Sloper is the name.
The quiet Chapel Lane, if exercise you need –
No problems have you here; two village seats are near.
On noticeboards it's clear, of matters of importance.
There is no need to cry if your petrol tank runs dry;
Sloper's garage always nigh to help you on your way.
Engines of steam so strong, WI half century gone,
Parish council been here years, among our souvenirs.

As the Shillingstone Song has it, Nobby Power, landlord at the Old Ox in the 1970s, was there "to keep in line with all the laws of drinking."

Long-serving Shillingstone WI member Mrs Pam Cole (right) planted the WI's millennium tree, a flowering cherry, beside the main road in December 1999. Looking on are WI President Mrs Christine Paul (left), and fellow members of the institute Mrs Lisa Hoghton and Mrs Moira Beddow.

66

Chapter 5

Working Ways

In keeping with other villages, Shillingstone followed the pattern of rural change with an increase in the number and variety of commercial outlets and trades over the 100 years from 1840 to 1940. During that period the population grew steadily from 512 to 582, but this was not as significant an influence for change as the technological advances and the consequent social developments.

Haymaking days at Laws Farm – when agriculture was still quite a major employer…

… and mechanisation, as in Marshall's threshing gear, was still relatively primitive.

In 1848, 10 specialist trades are listed in Kelly's Post Office Directories. There were nine owner farmers, including smallholders and, as was to be expected, agriculture was the chief occupation. At that time the village had four shopkeepers, two carpenters and two bootmakers. Others in single figures included a beer seller, a miller, a maltster, a smith, a publican and a tailor. By 1915, 20 different trades are listed, with several new ones appearing and a number from the 1848 list disappearing. During this period trades serviced the immediate locality. The numerous watermills illustrate the point, there being one each at Sturminster Newton, Fiddleford, Beremarsh and Durweston but by 1920 a number were no longer in use.

Similarly, local beer sellers gave way to the increase in pubs; one in 1859, two in 1867 and three in 1875 as commercial brewers replaced the cottage industries. However, people were often "Jacks of many trades" which presumably helped in times of change. John Trowbridge was designated stonemason, builder and decorator. Nearer the present day John Robins described himself as smallholder, water diviner, cider maker and insurance agent. His son, Lugeon Robins, of 2 Playcross, fondly remembered by some in the village, was employed by Mr Michael Pitt-Rivers as a painter but it was his cider combined with his generous sociable nature that impressed. It seems he was something of a joker. Poor Liza White, who was named the old witch by the children and who used to deliver the papers when not too drunk, was told by Lugeon that the sea was on fire at Bournemouth. Apparently she believed him and passed the rumour around the village. The "Tom Puds" and "Pippins" seem to have been responsible for many of the more interesting incidents in the village. The loss of Shillingstone's orchards might well be linked to the reduction in the number of outlandish village characters.

The 1860s and 70s were particularly significant in the way of change when in 1863 the Somerset and Dorset railway opened. The effect on the village was rapid and far-reaching. Two coal hauliers were established in the railway yard and, later, milk wholesalers and agricultural merchants opened offices and storage facilities.

The Crooked House with its shopfront. Eddie (Edwin) Sloper is standing in the doorway and standing guard over his wares are his son Ron and Jack Munday.

Sloper's Garage in the early days...

... and in 1965.

London came within reach for the "mossers," a trade that provided a good living for a number of men and women. One of them, Reg Read, was cagey however about the rewards for their labour. When asked, he replied: "Oh, sometimes more and sometimes less and nothing in between." The moss was pulled from the hillside and tied into small bundles and stocked 144 to a sack for which the mossers received £2. The moss was used in the funeral trade to line coffins and in the making of wreaths. During the First World War it was in demand for wound dressings.

Taking advantage of the line to London and Bournemouth, the Prideaux Milk factory opened in about 1900 at Cookswell. The milk was delivered by individual farms, processed and sent in churns by rail. Several men and women found work at this factory including a Mr Turvey who lived in The Anchorage (now Greensleeves). Every morning he was collected by a milk float loaded with churns, but because of his generous bulk he could not climb up so he simply perched, legs dangling, on the back. At lunchtime he retired across the road to the Seymer Arms and eventually returned to work somewhat less able. Jack Hart, another dairyman, well known for his attachment to the cider cask, was driving his milk float up Poplar Hill one day when his horse suddenly collapsed and died. Jack's immediate comment was reported to be: "Well, he never done that afore." The village relied on its wells and springs for its water supplies, and several are still in working order. A mains supply was introduced, however, when a diesel engine driving a ram was installed at Eastbrook Farm to lift water to a closed reservoir on the hillside above to be distributed from there around the village. The pump was the responsibility of Bill Beaumont who became know as Billy Bang Bang because of the noise the ram produced. His nickname continued through the family – his daughter being known as Nellie Bang.

By the turn of the century the motor car was making its presence felt. Edwin Sloper had established a shopfront in The Crooked House with cycle repairs and cycle hire at one penny per hour. By 1915 he developed this business into a garage offering petrol, repairs and car hire. The business expanded and was moved to the Slopers' orchard land alongside the Reading Room. In due course eight men were employed by the firm and the original tin shed was replaced by a larger building which was run by Ron Sloper, Edwin's son.

Peter Antell, who worked for Ron and who from an early age had a passion for heavy engines, bought the commercial part of the business in 1974, turning it into the biggest concern of its kind in Dorset. With the whole family actively involved in steam preservation and restoration, the building now takes on the look of a museum display of heavy commercial vehicles and steam engines.

Since then Sloper's Garage has changed hands several times, taking the name of Blandford Road Garage and, with a part change of use to a small supermarket. In 1984 Keith Fayers bought the car repair workshop, and the forecourt came into the hands of Cornwall Garages.

Power, whether steam or petrol, signalled the beginning of a more mobile society with all the advantages and drawbacks we now experience. 2 Maypole Terrace now a private house, illustrates some consequences of the change. Until the end of World War I the building was the workshop of Reg Robbins, a saddler, but as farming became increasingly mechanised and transport motorised there was little demand for this work. The shop was taken over by Mr Bennett who was described as a clothier but who sold many goods, including sweets, hardware and even fireworks. This in turn became a fruit and vegetable store run by James Farmiloe, who sold his shop in Blandford and developed a mobile shop serving customers in Blandford Forum and at Blandford Camp.

By 1940 the village had four shops – Howard England's bakery at Ivy House; Mr Jarrett's store at what is now the Post Office, and is now run by Keith and Julie Staddon; Sloper's cycle shop; and Stone and Rawles, whose grocery and drapery is now called Country Fayre or the Top Shop and which has become a small Londis supermarket run by the Pybus family. The latter was the original Post Office until Sydney Read's store took on the responsibility in the corner building at the top of Poplar Hill, opposite the school. That became the district Post Office and Sorting Office, serving a large rural area to the south-west of Shillingstone. Percy Butt's father, who lived at The Red House, walked daily out to Hazelbury Bryan, Woolland and Stoke Wake, delivering and collecting mail. For a brief period between the wars there was also a small butcher's shop run by Mr Garrett in the end of the cottages now called Greensleeves. As with other specialist retailers, meat was later supplied by a mobile shop serving several villages.

Paul Antell aboard Wally, the 1910 Robey of Lincoln traction engine he bought in 1969 and, with his father Peter, took 10 years to restore.

Walter Hart lived in the almshouses which used to stand next door to the Top Shop, repairing shoes and boots in his retirement. It is said that a pair of shoes left with him for repair at the outbreak of war in 1939 were still not ready in 1946. In those days people were not in such a hurry.

Robert Burgoyne, a carpenter and undertaker, had his premises at Ivy Cottage in Everetts Lane. Coffins were carried on an iron-wheeled bier that was pushed to church, often by a group of local boys. Mr Burgoyne followed in his black coat and top hat. Bardgy Hart took it upon herself to lay out the dead, greatly helped by an intake of alcoholic beverage. A very practical woman, she once sat her large weight on the lid of a coffin to close it because the corpse had, in her words, "swelled up so."

Other trades listed in 1939-40 included bootmaker, garage mechanic, blacksmith, three publicans, tailor, builders, hauliers, coal merchant, hay dealers, milk contractors, chalk quarrying and processing, cabinet maker, smallholder and even a dentist. The latter was Samuel Coniber whose surgery was in Cookswell cottages and who visited the village weekly.

By 1960 several of these village-based trades had gone as businesses became increasingly centralised in the towns. Some maintained a service as visiting mobile shops, such as Parker's the ironmonger, Hicks' clothiers – following a tradition established years earlier by the likes of Mr Dickenson who visited the village to sell pots and pans and buy rabbit and mole skins. Increasingly, as people bought cars, out-of-village shopping became possible and these mobile services declined.

Currently Shillingstone is fortunate in retaining in the village at least one pub, two shops, two garages and the services of several tradespeople such as builders, carpenters, painters and decorators.

It must come as a surprise to passers-by, though, when they see the sign "Oakford Oysters" some 20 miles inland, tucked away in a Dorset village. It is all to do with the Brewer family getting caught up with the Foyles. Not that there is anything "fishy" about that, more a case of "musselling in together"... As a result, some 107 acres of Poole harbour, leased from the Sea Fisheries Commission, became

71

The Shillingstone lime quarry – a landmark visible from miles around. Picture reproduced by courtesy of the Shillingstone Lime and Stone Co Ltd.

linked to a corner of the parish of Shillingstone. The name is a little misleading as the bulk of the business is concerned with the production of mussels. Five nights a week a lorryload sets out for Billingsgate market, the product of 18 months of "sea ranching." Farming would be the wrong word, as the double Poole tides do the feeding and nurturing after the tiny mussels have been seeded onto the mudflats. Given an 18-month growing period, they are harvested, graded and moved to Shillingstone where they self-clean in salt water for 42 hours. It sounds easy, but it is cold and wet work for the nine employees, and the mussels, just so that people can enjoy their moule marinière and a glass of Chablis.

Two other industries at Shillingstone have provided jobs for local people over the past century – on the hillside and, more recently, down in the old station yard. The lime quarry was started by Wilfred Bailey in 1924, digging out the chalk initially with a pick and shovel, his only other equipment being a wheelbarrow and a motor-cycle and sidecar. Agricultural chalk was supplied for farming, and quicklime for the building trade in a rapidly expanding Bournemouth. Two of the kilns which were fired up at the outset to produce the quicklime – in the traditional way dating back to Roman times – were burning continuously for more than 75 years until they were finally extinguished at the end of 1999. It was by then the last remaining site in Britain where hydrated lime was still being produced in this way, and it was much in demand for the mortar used in restoring old buildings. The Bailey family – sons Leslie and Eric took over running the business from their father – held the turbary (turf) and mineral rights to a large part of the hill above Shillingstone until they sold the quarry in 1989. After that it continued to trade as the Shillingstone Lime and Stone Co Ltd for another 10 years. On the market again at the beginning of the new millennium, one option under consideration was to close down the quarry which has become a familiar landmark visible from the air and from miles around, and build a country house on the site. But because of its geological importance the quarry has been designated a Site of Special Scientific Interest so whatever happens there is a requirement to keep at least part of the face exposed for future study.

Just as the coming of the railway brought fundamental changes in the village, so its closure caused other changes. The vacant railway yard was occupied first by Pilgrim's, a firm that produced poultry housing and equipment, together with domestic furniture. Later came a motor-cycle repair shop; and in the old station buildings a model railway engineering company that is now in Child Okeford. Following the precedent set by Pilgrim's, larger businesses were established including Resislek, Inlays and Hambledon Furniture. Then in 1981 Intasco took over the site, employing about 100 people in the production of replica antique furniture and thereby continuing a trade that started when the last railway lines were lifted in 1966. The succession of change continued when in 1996 Intasco sold out to a national company. They maintained production under the name of Casterbridge Furniture until 1998 when they were no longer able to compete against cheap imports from the Far East – so even tiny Shillingstone has felt the impact of the new global economy. One wonders what will feature in another Shillingstone book at the close of the next century, never mind the next millennium.

For the present, however, there is still some less global, more local continuity. Several families, over a long period of time, have maintained their links with particular trades. The name Melmoth appears in Kelly's Directories as a carpenter from 1840 until 1930. Similarly, the Jacksons were tailors from 1880 until Fred Jackson died in 1960. The name Cox has been associated with Lambs House Farm (now called Hambledon Farm) since 1848 and, during the same period, the Store family appeared under a variety of trades, first as smiths and later as carpenters and publicans in the New Ox.

Over the years, though, there has been a steady increase in the number of people classified as "private residents." This term suggests "people of consequence" – those who have no need to work or have retired. Names of widows and a few widowers, plus some retired couples who previously appeared as tradespeople, feature in this list. Not having to work until you dropped used to be something of a luxury.

A workplace of the 1920s – the milk factory (now the premises of Dee Jays Motor Sales), opposite the Seymer Arms (now the Silent Whistle).

Men at work – bringing main drainage to Shillingstone in 1949.

 **Chapter 6**

Railway Lines

– some points from between the tracks

Shillingstone railway station, on the Somerset and Dorset line, opened on 31st August 1863. It was the beginning of a lifeline for the people of Shillingstone.

One S&D driver, Bert White, recalls King Edward VII alighting here to visit Lord Ismay at Iwerne Minster House (now Clayesmore School), and after his first visit Shillingstone became a "first class station" with a platform canopy added, and all stationmasters from then on having gold braid embroidered on their caps.

❖   ❖   ❖   ❖

BOE Downes began work on the S&D on 1st May 1962 as a porter at Shillingstone with its two platforms, 16-lever signalbox and goods yard. During his first week, in the company of a regular porter, he had to change the signal lamps. The "up home" was the shortest of the main signals at about 15 feet; the "up distant", "down distant" and "down starter" were much higher, while the "up starter" was 45 foot high at the top of a 30-foot bank. So when it was wet and windy this could be very dangerous work (they used to sway in the wind). "I wonder what the health and safety people would say today about having to climb up a 40-foot ladder with a lamp in one's hand and no guard rail," said Mr Downes. "It used to petrify me as I could not stand heights."

On one summer's day he had a different kind of fright. Walking along the track to the "down distant" he was enjoying the Dorset countryside, not listening out for

Shillingstone station in about 1910.

75

anything and feeling pretty good when suddenly he heard a metallic clank behind him. "Turning round quickly I was faced with a light engine bearing down on me a matter of yards away. I jumped out of its path in record time. The footplate crew had not seen me. Thank goodness for worn big ends on the Fowler engines – it saved my life! Normally there were no train movements after the 14.38 until the 15.25 down milk from Templecombe."

Another day, after replacing the "up distant" lamps and returning past the gangers hut a voice called out: "Hey, Bob." Two gangers, Don Bradley and Joe Duffet were in the hut enjoying a drop of scrumpy. "Do you want some?" they asked. "Not one to look a gift horse in the mouth I went in and had two very small flask cups of very sweet thick syrupy scrumpy (nectar) made just along the track by Lugeon Robins. On leaving the hut to walk back to the station – I had to catch the down Milky – in the warm sun the cider began to take effect. Nearing the 'up home' signal my train ran in. Well, two trains ran in – I was seeing double. I had to put the lamp in the shed, collect my bike and run over to the down platform and get on the milk train. Luckily the footplate crew waited for me."

SCRUMPY always reminds Mr Downes of Harry Guy, "a marvellous old goods porter at Shillingstone." If he helped out on the platform and got a shilling tip (5p) from a passenger, as soon as the coast was clear he would nip over to the Seymer Arms for a pint of scrumpy. In winter he would have his pint drawn, put it in a saucepan and warm it on the pub's open fire.

Shillingstone station was almost on a par with Midsomer Norton for its flower gardens, climbing roses and lawns. The small greenhouse at the southern end of the platform was where the staff grew seedlings right up to 1965 for transplanting into the borders. Everything was kept neat and tidy right up till the line closed in March 1966. Near the greenhouse was a rosebush with a wonderful scent which on a warm day could be smelt at the other end of the platform. This bush was generally maintained by one of the regular passenger guards, Albert (Dickie) Bird. He would always have a rose in his buttonhole and carried a pruning knife in his pocket at all times. He would tend the rose while the porters unloaded any parcels and when the train was ready to go he would say: "One more snip." He would then get back on the train, shout out: "Right away, driver," give a smile and a wave to everybody and the train would be on its way to Sturminster Newton. He did not know what this rose was called but when he grew one himself he named it "Shillingstone." He was a fine man and well liked by staff and passengers.

Most of the guards were friendly and were always ready for a laugh and a joke Mr Downes recalled, for instance, Leonard Rossiter, Cyril Martin and Bill Mills.

DURING the morning the porters loaded lorries as well as unloading cattle feed from the rail wagons. Ted Drew would come down from Sturminster Newton as would Mervyn Allen or Joe Symes from Blandford with his Thornycroft 10-ton lorry. Mr Downes would sometimes go out with Mr Symes who would be driving along briskly at all of 20mph. When about to go down a hill he would say: "Pull the trailer brake on a couple of notches to slow us down." They would slow to about 5mph which was necessary because although the tractor unit had brakes the tractor was only fitted with a hand-operated brake to the trailer. And this was 1962. Shillingstone also had its own lorry driver, the last one being Rodney Galpin. Before him were Bert Sherlock and Bob Downes' uncle Frank Downes.

THE first passenger train down through Shillingstone in the morning carried cream to the hotels in Bournemouth and Poole from the local dairy of Edward Phillips. Some mornings there were as many as 12 churns of different sizes which could be quite heavy for one man to push on the trolley. Invariably some of the male passengers would lend a helping hand up the slope. Some mornings when Wilf Savory was on duty he would ask the goods porter Harry Guy to see the cream onto the train. This meant only one thing. Leonard Rossiter was the guard and the two of them would pull each others' legs and sparks used to fly, but all in good fun.

Other traffic included live rams from Mr Tory's farm at Turnworth. He or one of the farmhands would bring a ram over to the station to send off for stud purposes to other farms all over the country. Sometimes it was difficult leading the rams over to the down platform, so the porters would sit astride them with their feet on the ground and steer them by their horns.

RECALLING the winter of 1962-63, Mr Downes said: "Nothing could move; even tractors could not get through. On the Monday I set off from my home, Littleton Farm. I couldn't get to Shillingstone station because of the drifting snow so I struggled the two miles across the fields to Blandford which was my 'senior

BR Class 5 No 73001 at Shillingstone with one of the last holiday excursion trains on the S&D, on 30th August 1965. Fireman John Sawyer is leaning out of the cab.

station' to report for duty. I spent all day shovelling snow off the station platform. I carried this out for a couple of days and on the third day made it to Shillingstone and resumed my duties there. But again most of my work was clearing snow off the platforms.

"The space between the platforms was level, with snow three feet deep. Eventually a snowplough got through from Templecombe. I had to cycle nine miles from home, with hazardous lumps of ice on the road that stayed until April. I parked my bike in the waiting room in front of the blazing coal fire to thaw out the gears which were encased in ice.

"Some nights Alan Cox the signalman and I would sleep in the signalbox. We would have the stove red hot, with the kettle continually boiling for making hot drinks. Even so the inside of the windows still iced up. The draught through the windows was pretty bad despite covering the frame with the signalbox carpet The easterly wind came across the meadows and river and into the bottom of the box and up through the frame. After a few days the water supply froze up; it was pretty desperate.

The signalbox where Bob Downes recalls some icy draughts – and some tasty Saturday night fry-ups.

"Numerous times each day we and the technical staff from Blandford had to

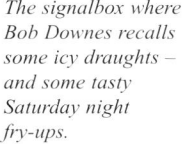

unfreeze the points and dig them out again. It was a constant battle for almost three months. When the thaw came it was very welcome. Just below the station the Stour was frozen solid. When the water started to run again the ice flows started to move. Some were as big as 20 feet across, bringing down bushes and trees. About a quarter of a mile downstream was a footbridge over the river. The continuous grinding and buffeting by the ice flows took the bridge downstream with them."

All the staff thought that because the S&D had coped so well, where road transport could not, the Transport Minister might have second thoughts about closure.

IT was a lovely way of life working on the S&D in the early 1960s, said Mr Downes, but a as it was coming to an end. "Saturday evenings at Shillingstone station were fry-up time. We would bring sausages, bacon, eggs and bread, and pick mushrooms in the nearby fields. At times there were 10 of us in the signalbox munching away. And during the summer holidays the river bank could be quite crowded with local people of all ages, some swimming, others picnicking. We would often have a quick dip to cool off between trains."

After the demise of through traffic and goods trains in late 1964 the staff had a lot of free time between trains, so more time was devoted to keeping Shillingstone station clean, polishing all the brasswork, tending the flowerbeds and transplanting seedlings from the greenhouse into the borders. Built into the down platform shelter was a small room where all the station records were kept. "Once or twice we burnt a lot of this paper," said Mr Downes. "How we wish we had kept it."

For many years at the beginning and end of each school term the local public schools – Hanford, Croft House and Clayesmore – would receive and despatch the children's trunks, tuckboxes and other luggage. It was a very busy time and a good provider of revenue. Unfortunately, though, because of rumours of closure of the line the schools withdrew their custom from the railways during 1963 and sent their pupils and luggage by coach instead, which was another nail in the coffin of the S&D. The county council also withdrew concessions for the grammar school children from Sturminster Newton and Shillingstone and laid on buses for them.

"By 1966," said Mr Downes sadly, "the S&D that I knew and worked on was coming to an end. Looking back from 33 years on, I should have loved it even more. It was goodbyes to goods porter Nobby Whiting, signalmen Jim Maidment and John Cluett, porter Ivor Bickle and crossing keeper Fred Andrews."

ENGINE driver Reg Darke remembers losing his fireman on one trip. They had left with the Bournemouth to Bath train and arrived at Blandford. The engine had a high tender and a double door which you could clamber up through allowing you to push the coal forward. Reg had an agile young fireman called Mervyn Beltin. After taking on water and securing the flexible pipe to the water column,

Fellow S&D railway workers gathered to give signalman George Ainsworth a send-off into retirement on 18th December 1965. He had worked on the line for over 50 years, mostly at Shillingstone. With him and his wife Cicely are Bert Scammell, Don May, Reg Eaton, Wilf Savory, Len Farley, Ken Forrester, Bill Dyer, Jack Bell, Alan Cox, Ivor Ridout, Bob Downes, Donald Ridout, Roy Yates, Ron Jackson and Jim Maidment.

the driver expected his fireman to appear through the tender doors. So he opened up the power and made off to Shillingstone. He glanced back into the cab and realised there was no fireman. To stop the train would have caused much delay. Looking back at the front carriage, there was his fireman waving for all his worth.

At Shillingstone the sheepish fireman got back into the cab. He had popped off the engine for a glass of water and just about made it into the carriage as the train was moving off. The women who had been to Blandford for their shopping were highly amused that the train's fireman was sitting with them in their carriage.

ERIC Miles, a former S&D signalman, remembered his holidays in the 1920s when he was a youngster. When arriving at Shillingstone station for his one-day holiday a year to Bournemouth, it was a thrill to get his ticket stamped in a machine. He crossed the line to the down side of the platform listening to the bells jingling in the signalbox, little realising that many years later he would become a signalman on the S&D himself. The train would arrive. There were no corridor coaches, a toilet would be shared between the compartments, sepia pictures of holiday spots adorned the walls above the seats. He remembered the emergency cord with a notice of a £5 fine if pulled unnecessarily, the leather strap for lowering the window, the enjoyment of watching the stations go by, and, on arrival at Bournemouth, heading off to the beach for a day of fun. How things have changed.

THE closure of the S&D had a devastating effect as reporter Alan Rogers wrote in a local newspaper. The 1,000 villagers of Shillingstone, Dorset, lost their station on Saturday 5th March 1966 when the last train made its way from Bath to Bournemouth on the Somerset and Dorset line, affectionately known to passengers as the "Slow and Dirty."

The closure made getting to work more difficult. Kathleen Rose, who was 21 at the time, worked as a chemist's assistant in Sturminster Newton. The bus services did not fit her hours. She either cycled or on wet days took a taxi which cost her 7s 6d. Eventually she tired of the inconvenience and took another job at a grocers in her own village. Charles Coles, the village chimney sweep, lived in Sturminster Newton and put his bicycle on the train to get to Shillingstone. Aged 64, he had to cycle 10 miles to and from work instead, and on average got round two houses fewer per day. So his earnings dropped by some £5 a week.

One of the reasons Geoffrey Popplewell left his teaching job at a preparatory school 16 miles from Shillingstone was the difficulty of getting there. His wife Isabel taught at a school 17 miles in a different direction and normally drove there in the family car. In bad weather she preferred to travel by bus but then arrived 30 minutes before the school opened. She had to wait four hours for the bus home.

Trade was hit too. Village tradesmen found that the last post went at 4.30pm instead of 6.20pm so that late orders and letters missed it. Delivery of certain goods became a problem as well. Garage proprietor Ronald Sloper had to send a vehicle almost every day to fetch spare parts which were previously delivered by train from the surrounding towns.

As things were shortly before the Somerset and Dorset line closed...

Isolation of the elderly was one of the more upsetting results of the rail closure. Mabel Candy, aged 66, had been in the habit of visiting her invalid sister at Corfe Castle every two months or so. Because the buses were unsuitable, her only way of making the trip was to rely on other relatives so she had to cut her visits to once every four or five months.

And Eveline Tate said: "I just don't go anywhere now because I don't want to keep bothering my relatives."

RAILWAY STAFF RECALLED AT SHILLINGSTONE STATION

Signalmen – George Ainsworth, William Lanning, Jim Maidment, Alan Cox, John Cluett,
Harold Hooper, brothers Bert and Harry Scammell, Bob McKinney.

Stationmasters – Mr Courage, Ken Davey, Ken Forrester, Albert Powis, Sidney Cox.

Porters – Bob Downes, Harry Guy, Percy Ladd, Ivor Bickle, Wilf Savory, Reg Eaton,
Derek Levens, Dennis Cockburn.

Booking clerk – Don Ridout.

Lorry drivers – Bert Sherlock, Rodney Galpin, Frank Downes.

Gangers – Albert Snook, Joe Duffet.

The last train has gone. The station remains ... but in a sorry state now.

SHILLINGSTONE

FATAL ACCIDENT AT THE STATION

CHECKER'S SAD DEATH

THE headlines in *The Western Gazette* of 5th January 1912 told the story of this tragedy in nine words. It took a full broadsheet column of small print, however, to reveal in grim and minute detail why "quite a gloom was cast over this locality on new year's day."

Samuel Crane, a checker employed at Shillingstone railway station for some 20 years, was 41 years old. He was, said the report of the inquest, "well known by a large number of the public who travel through this station, and was much esteemed by all on account of his studious attention to passengers and his cheery disposition." He was chairman of the parish council and left a widow and eight children, "the majority of whom are of tender years."

The inquest held in the Church room on Tuesday 2nd January 1912 was conducted by the coroner, Mr W H Creech. Mr A Holland was foreman of the jury which returned a verdict of accidental death and declared that no officials or railway staff were in any way to blame.

Witnesses had told the inquest about what happened when the 3.20pm up train from Bournemouth to Bath that Monday arrived at Shillingstone where a horsebox it had picked up in Blandford was due to be dropped off at the bridge just beyond the station. Mr Crane, who was responsible for the uncoupling at the bridge, rode on the outside steps of the wagon to that point. No one saw precisely how it happened, but he must have slipped and fallen off, to be struck by some part of the train causing the severe head injuries from which he died a matter of hours later.

Among those who gave evidence at the inquest were George Savory and Richard Spencer, manager and assistant manager respectively of Messrs Smart and Son's coalyard at the station, stationmaster Robert Ames, porter John Marsh, train driver Thomas Hardacre and guard Abraham Hamblin, and Dr Newbould from Child Okeford who was sent for by the stationmaster and arrived on the scene just after 4pm.

The coroner said Samuel Crane was held in the highest respect by everybody and was generally liked. His untimely death was a matter for deep regret not only to the station staff but also to the villagers and the travelling public, of whom Mr Creech said he was one. He added: "It was a sad accident, especially coming as it did at the start of a new year, and must be a terrible blow to those who were near and dear to him."

Mr Ames said that during the 18 years Mr Crane had been under him "he had found him to be a good servant, honest, straightforward and a good workman."

Further high tributes were paid at the funeral service which, as reported in *The Western Gazette* the following week, took place in Shillingstone "in the presence of a large gathering of parishioners and friends" – and railway colleagues from up and down the Somerset and Dorset line from Blandford to Bath. The service conducted by the Rector, the Rev Dr Cooke, was "fully choral, the singing being led by the surpliced choir." Floral tributes came from "relatives and many of the gentry in the locality."

The Rector, in his address, "pointed out the lessons to be learnt from such a sudden calamity as had befallen the deceased, and said it showed everyone the great necessity of being prepared."

Shillingstone's other railway

Meriel Lady Salt recalls how her pig-farming husband Sir Tom Salt came to build the railway that encircled their home, Shillingstone House:

Back in the late 1940s and early 50s Sir Tom had a small Fergie tractor which occasionally got stuck in the mud as the land was so boggy, and he had to call on neighbouring farmers to come and pull him out. One particularly bad day three other tractors as well as his own were all stuck trying to help one another. That decided it. "I'm going to build a railway," he announced.

It took 10 years to construct the narrow-gauge line, with over a mile of track, down past the pigsties to the field beside Puxey Lane and back up through a cutting to the engine sheds and turntable. Designed principally as a working line for the farm, a flatbed truck was used to carry the feed to the pigs, another deep-sided truck was used for moving the pigs and a dual-purpose one was either used for cleaning out the straw from the sties or it had seats which could be installed to carry passengers. A custom-built open carriage, with first-class and second-class seating, was hitched to the train when it was used as an attraction at fêtes held in the garden of Shillingstone House.

The first engine Sir Tom used was diesel-powered, with a cab large enough for an adult to sit inside. A more powerful diesel locomotive was acquired later, and in the early 1960s a magnificent steam engine – a scaled-down version of the kind to be seen in Africa and South America with a double tender, tall chimney and gleaming brass dome. Sadly, he had little time to enjoy that one because he died in 1965.

Some 10 years later the end of the line was reached for this railway track through Shillingstone, despite efforts by some of the redundant Somerset and Dorset staff to keep it going. Not much sign is left of it apart from remnants of the station and the level crossing at the top of the drive. But then that was one good reason in Sir Tom's mind when he built it – when it was no longer needed the track and sleepers and gravel could be removed and within a year it would all revert to nature, whereas if he had put in concrete roads they would still be a blot on the landscape.

Chapter 7

The Religious Life

The Parish Church of the Holy Rood

Where in Shillingstone would you find a letter from a king, a memento to the Great Plague of 1665 and a coffin perhaps 1,300 years old? The answer is, of course, in the oldest building in Shillingstone, the Church of the Holy Rood, parts of which may date from the last years of the 11th century.

No one knows when the first Shillingstone church was built. We know that a missionary bishop was very active in the area in the last half of the seventh century and the existence of Saxon remains around the churchyard indicate that there must have been a church building here about that time – probably destroyed, as many were, by fire and war.

Shillingstone would have been a reasonably sized village when the present church was built – about 45 men and a total population of about 230 – and early priests were appointed by a monastery and lay patronage. So for a good deal of its early history, until 1600, Shillingstone continued to have two Rectors, none of whom lived in the village for much of the time and some of whom were exceedingly quarrelsome with each other – a fine example to the parishioners. When the church was under the care of one Rector things were not always much better. One 19th century rector was absent so often he was told by the Bishop to choose between his hunting and his church. He chose his hunting. Another 18th century Rector, Peter Brodie, was presented to the living in 1777 but never appeared at all.

Shillingstone Church.

Shillingstone's Church of the Holy Rood on a postcard dated 1912. The four lime trees on the left have grown up in the intervening 88 years, and so has the cedar on the right.

He, therefore, does not appear on the list in the church of Shillingstone incumbents.

The men who built Shillingstone church in the 11th and 12th centuries would certainly not recognise it today. It was originally a small square building to which the chancel and the sanctuary were added (13th century), then the bell tower (15th century) and finally the north aisle in 1888. The bell tower acquired a clock in 1897 to celebrate Queen Victoria's diamond jubilee and this was restored to sparkling splendour in good time for the millennium. The north aisle itself has seen many changes since it was added. The vestry has moved up and down the church and the area which was once full of pews is now an open space after the reordering of the interior in January 1992. As originally there would have been no seats in the church at all, perhaps the creation of the open space returned the church more to its original appearance.

The ring of five bells in the parish church were removed in 1929 for rehanging, for a new bellchamber floor to be fitted and for the treble to be recast… at a cost of £387 14s as indicated by the bill dated 14th October 1929 from the bell founders, John Taylor and Co, of Loughborough. The sixth bell was not added until nine years later, in 1938 in memory of Canon Dayman.

The striking features today include the small Norman windows, efficient for light and economical for heat. There is also the Jacobean pulpit, probably given in 1666 by William Keen in thanksgiving for his deliverance from the plague. He was able to escape from London and stay in the village until the plague had passed, and the Great Fire of London which followed it. The pulpit used to have a canopy but this had disappeared some 200 years later – maybe firewood in the village was scarce during one hard winter.

The church bells, five to begin with but six now, still ring out every Sunday and on as many other occasions as possible provided there is sufficient excuse. The largest bell, the tenor, weighs 15cwt, 2qrtrs and 9lbs and rings in the key of E.

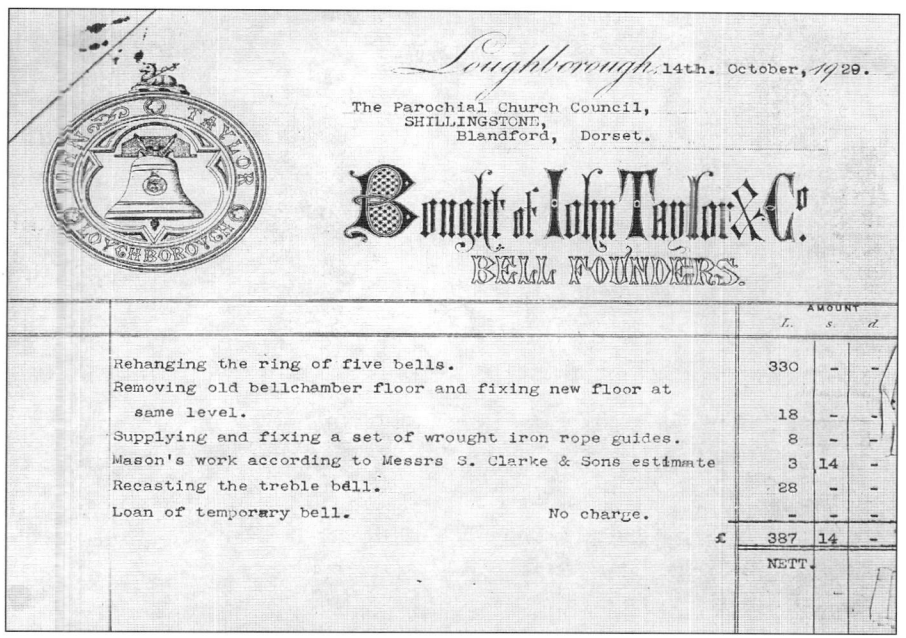

Loughborough, 14th. October, 1929.

The Parochial Church Council,
SHILLINGSTONE,
Blandford, Dorset.

Bought of Iohn Taylor & Co.

BELL FOUNDERS.

	£	s.	d.
Rehanging the ring of five bells.	330	–	–
Removing old bellchamber floor and fixing new floor at same level.	18	–	–
Supplying and fixing a set of wrought iron rope guides.	8	–	–
Mason's work according to Messrs S. Clarke & Sons estimate	3	14	–
Recasting the treble bell.	28	–	–
Loan of temporary bell. No charge.			
£	387	14	–
NETT.			

The oldest known bell was cast in 1622 but recast in 1892 and the original bells still in position, the fifth and the tenor, date from 1736. The sixth and last bell, the treble, was added in 1938 in memory of Canon Dayman.

There is also the magnificent ceiling of the nave and chancel painted by, or certainly under the direction of G H Bodley, an eminent church architect associated with William Morris. The rood screen, purchased from another church in 1902 and pictured in many early photographs, only survived for some 75 years – it seems to have been widely, although not totally disliked.

The interior of the parish church showing the rood screen, the Jacobean pulpit to the right, part of the north aisle on the left, the nave's painted ceiling, and the old oil lamps.

The parish church choir and other members of the congregation with the Rev Dr J H Cooke in about 1927.

The choir in the late 1920s, with organist and choirmaster Mr Popham.

There are many other treasures of which the church is custodian. The most poignant might well be the letter from King George V congratulating the village on its magnificent response to Kitchener's call to join the Colours in the First World War. Shillingstone was a community of brave people and there are still some left at the beginning of the new millennium who watched their loved ones leave for the Somme, or Mons, or Paeschendale, never to return. Also kept in the church is a framed piece of gun metal, the remnant of the gun presented to Shillingstone in 1919 in recognition of its brave volunteers, but sacrificed for the cause of munitions in the Second World War.

Look around the church and find the magnificent brass eagle lectern presented in memory of the Rev Dr J H Cooke and still painstakingly polished every week. In the present vestry there is also a wonderful sculpture by Sir Francis Chantrey of Elizabeth Acton, the young curate's wife who died aged 29 in 1917. And still in use is a silver chalice from the reign of Elizabeth I.

Reminders in the parish church of Croft House School include the memorial to the founders, Lt-Col and Mrs Torkington, and stained glass from the old school chapel.

Many worshippers today would say that other treasures are Holy Rood's fine choral and musical tradition. The organ was bought from Iwerne Minster church

*A Count of Money Disbursted
by James Cox, Churchwarden,
in the Year of Our Lord 1817*

	£	s	d
Paid at Visitation	1	3	0
Paid the Parson at Visitation		10	6
Paid for Bred and Wine		6	1½
To ye Lond at Visitation		14	0
Paid for Mending the Clock Rope		0	6
Paid for Bred and Wine		5	10½
Paid the Ringers Gunpowderplot		5	0
Paid for Parchment		6	0
Paid for Cleaning the Clock		6	0
Paid the Blacksmithes Bill		2	6
Paid for Bred Wine		5	11½
Paid the Maseners Bill	2	17	6½
Paid for Beer for the Maseners		7	0
Paid for A Bell Rope		9	0
Paid for Bred and Wine		5	11½
For Fetching 10 Lods of Gravel		6	0
Pd for Mending the Whele Barrow			
& Pail Broken at the Church		4	0
Paid the Clarks Fees	2	10	0
Paid for Drawing up the Clock	1	1	
Paid for Washing the Surples 5 Times		13	0
Paid for Washing the Pall & Table Linen		2	6
Paid for Treming the Church Yard		6	0
Paid for Oil for the Clock		3	0
Paid the Carpentors Bill		10	9
	14	1	2½

A churchwarden's expenses account in 1817 – the gist of it and the bottom line of £14 1s 2½d are clear enough even if the spelling does leave something to be desired.

One of Shillingstone's "high churchmen"... The Rev Noel Palmer, who stood about 6ft 6in tall, was Rector from 1947 to 1953.

in 1913 for £130. It was restored in 1998 at a cost of £6,000.

At the turn of the millennium the church was still using the baptism register begun with Frank Hallet on 23rd May 1869 and the burial register dating from the entry of Louisa Cox on 1st June 1902. Other records of village births, marriages and deaths go back to 1654, but earlier registers have unfortunately been lost or destroyed. There are undoubtedly some very early tombs in the churchyard, dating from the 7th or 8th centuries and the Saxon head of St Birinius, or perhaps Jesus, greets you above the church door. But the earliest recorded burial in the churchyard is that of Thomas Hare on 17th May 1654.

Shillingstone church's most striking feature of all, however, is its living presence as a holy place for the worship of God. There continues to be a lively and flourishing congregation but the atmosphere of calm and peace which everyone discovers on entering is the result of hundreds of years of worship and prayer. Having survived at least one millennium Holy Rood, Shillingstone, is well equipped to proclaim God's living presence through another.

The Methodist Chapel

Charmouth, in the south-western extremity of Dorset, in the year 1640 was the residence of the village parson, Bartholomew Westley, the great-grandfather of the founder of Methodism. Parson Westley was, like his famous great-grandchildren obviously unhappy with the formal worship of the Church of England and in 1660 at the time of the Restoration he was ejected from his rectories of Charmouth and Catherstone. It seems he sustained himself and his family precariously by the practice of medicine. This humble man walked a rough and thorny path, until one day the tidings of his son's death reached him and then "his heart broke" and the grey-headed confessor passed to his unknown grave.

In 1658 and in a village much nearer Shillingstone, John Westley, son of Bartholomew and grandfather of the Wesley brothers, became the successful minister to the village of Winterborne Whitechurch. (His grandson's journal records him as saying to the Bishop of Bristol: "It pleased God to seal my labours with success in the apparent conversion of many souls.") However, in 1662 as he was coming out of church one Sunday, John Westley was arrested through the bitter malice of his enemies and hurried away to Blandford gaol. He was released shortly afterwards and returned to Winterborne Whitechurch for a few months; and then the Act of Uniformity which prescribed the form of public prayers, administration of the sacraments and other rites in the Church of England came into force and on 17th August 1662 Minister Westley left his church for the last time. During the last five years of his life John Westley was an itinerant preacher.

He is thought to have died in 1670 but the place of his burial cannot accurately be ascertained.

One is left to speculate whether this great man who preached "just over the hill" in Winterborne Whitechurch was known personally, or by reputation, in Shillingstone and whether in his travels he ever preached to the nonconformists of this village.

In the middle of the 18th century the grandsons of Mr John Westley, John and Charles Wesley, began the evangelical Methodist movement and, nearly 200 years after Mr Westley preached in Winterborne Whitechurch, the earliest recorded chapel in Shillingstone was built in 1854-55 for £120. The tithe maps for that period show that the chapel was in Hine Town Lane. An Order for the Shaftesbury Circuit dated 1866 shows that two services were held in Shillingstone on a Sunday, at 2.30pm and 6pm, and once a month a service was held at 7pm on a Tuesday. Preachers would have come, some by horse and some no doubt on foot, from as far afield as Shaftesbury, Gillingham, Sturminster Newton and Blandford. In 1866 Shillingstone joined the newly formed Blandford and Sturminster Circuit. No record is known of the membership of the village chapel, but in 1870 it is recorded that within the circuit there were two ministers, 24 local preachers and the membership amounted to 306 in the 13 chapels.

The chapel in Blandford Road was built in 1904 at a cost of £805 and in due course became part of the Stour Valley mission. An order of services for the fourth quarter of 1963 shows that two Sunday services were still held at the chapel, though the times had changed to 11am and 6pm. Two services on a Wednesday at 7.15pm are listed for the quarter. During October, November and December 1963 preachers came from Blandford, Sturminster Newton, Kinson and Milton Abbas, presumably coming now by car. On the Sunday before Christmas 1963 Mr K G Harvey of Sturminster Newton preached in the morning and Mr E R Sloper of Shillingstone preached in the evening. There is no record of a service being held on Christmas Day. However, it should be noted that there was a united service at the chapel on 29th Sunday December 1963 when the Rector of Holy Rood Church preached.

The Methodist Chapel beside the main road through Shillingstone.

After 213 recorded years of Methodist worship in the Shillingstone chapel the doors were finally closed in 1995. The arguments that forced John Westley from his church in 1662 are now long mended and once a month the village Methodists are welcomed into the Church of the Holy Rood for their own form of worship.

The redundant chapel was used for a time as a base for restoring good-quality second-hand furniture, for resale at very low prices to those in the area who were on benefits and who, without this furniture, would have had nothing in their homes. When this business expanded and moved to larger premises the chapel was put on the market.

The Gospel Hall

Reginald Carnell, an Elder of the Shillingstone Brethren, leads the worship in Shillingstone's Gospel Hall which was started in 1928 in a purpose-built hut by Samuel Robbins, of Sunnybank, Shillingstone. The present hall was built on the same site about two years later by Mr S Clarke, of Sturminster Newton.

There were many members at that time who played their part. Preachers also came most Sundays from other areas.

Frank Cains, a well-known gardener in the village, took the Sunday School for many years, followed by Charlie Butt who was also a very faithful member.

Chapter 8

School Days

If you had been born in Shillingstone 150 years ago would you have been able to do joined-up writing by the age of 10? The answer is easy; you would probably not even have been able to write your own name. The 1851 census described Martha Hart, aged 26, as a "schoolmistress," but not a single child was described as a "scholar." James Jackson, aged nine, and James Percy, Mark Courage and William Hart, all 10, were "farm boys," Mary Arnold and Sarah Candy, both 12, were "servants," Christiana Jeffrey, aged 14, was a "needlewoman." One of the thatchers in the village, William Rollings, was 13. The vast majority of the children probably helped their parents in the fields and gardens, or with the washing – not as easy as it sounds. Perhaps, if they were very lucky, they might have learned something at a "dame school."

Hutchins, the Dorset historian, wrote of Shillingstone in 1874: "There is a Church of England school, built by the present Rector (Canon Dayman), AD1854, but there were originally two dame schools in the village, one at Lanchard and one opposite the new chapel."

We know nothing about the dame schools although, interestingly, Canon Dayman records the burial in 1864 of Jane Savery whom he describes in Latin as "once a schoolmistress." She had been found dead one morning after falling into a ditch in her orchard and the tithe map shows that she lived near the Methodist chapel. Perhaps, like other "dames," she provided in her parlour some education for the children of the poor in Shillingstone. The marriage registers show that roughly two out of three men who married between 1837 and 1860 could write their names; the proportion of brides who could do so was slightly higher. The proportions remained much the same during the next decade but illiteracy became very rare after 1880.

Other than dame schools there was no education to be had in rural England except that provided by two religious societies. The National Society had been established in 1811 by Andrew Bell and the bishops of the Church of England. Like his rival, the Quaker Joseph Lancaster who founded the British and Foreign Society, Bell used the older children – the monitors – to teach the younger ones. This system was cheap to run – there was need for only one teacher who taught the monitors – and both societies were short of money. Most of the younger children learned parrot fashion with little real understanding and, to start with, the quality of the education seemed not to matter very much.

In 1833 Parliament granted £20,000 a year "for the purposes of education." The money was shared by the two societies and used to build schools but, although the annual grant had risen to £500,000 by the middle of the century, rural areas had to wait until the crowded industrial towns had been catered for. Shillingstone waited until 1854 when, according to some loose notes in the school logbook, Canon Dayman built the school on land which was part of the Beckford Estate. Lord Rivers, who owned what later became the Portman Estate, was a tenant for life of the land on which the school stands, and he approved the idea of a school. He gave Canon Dayman permission to commandeer the plot and hold it rent free for the necessary period of 20 years in order to gain "Squatter's Title." He also contributed money, as did many of the Shillingstone Rector's friends and relations.

We know very little about the school until 1862 when Maria Bacon, the mistress, began to keep in a logbook, as ordered by the Government, a bare record of events with details of weekly attendance figures and fees paid. She was a certified teacher – the Government had set up a framework of training colleges, with school inspectors to ensure that teachers were doing their job properly. When a Royal Commission discovered that only a tiny minority of the children who went to school really did learn the three Rs it was decided that schools which were not achieving good results should lose some of their funding.

This "payment by results" policy has been described as stultifying. Imagine the panic of the teacher-in-charge – Maria Bacon, for instance – when the date of the inspection was announced. She was 23 and had been born in Wells. She lodged with William Melmoth, carpenter, and his wife Charity. Three of the Melmoths' children went to the village school and are described as "scholars" in the 1861 census, as were over 100 other children between the ages of four and 15. Many of them went to school rarely, it seems, because the highest attendance recorded by Maria Bacon was 76. Perhaps it was just as well because there was only one classroom, albeit with a gallery.

Miss Bacon had some help in the shape of Margaret Adams, pupil teacher, who was then 16. The system of apprenticing prospective teachers for five years to a headmaster or headmistress had been introduced in 1846. They could then go on at the age of 17 or so to a teacher-training school for one, two or three years. Her Majesty's Inspectors checked each year on the standards reached in the three Rs, and teachers' salaries were affected if a poor standard resulted in a reduction of the grant. Margaret Adams left the school in 1864 "not liking to go on under the new code" and was succeeded by Elizabeth Melmoth, daughter of Miss Bacon's landlord, then aged 12.

The inspector's report for 1867 was disparaging. "The school is in a fair state of general efficiency... the sums are not done so neatly and readily as they might be... the lower classes are very backward." And of Elizabeth Melmoth: "Her religious knowledge, arithmetic and grammar need special attention." Miss Bacon must have guessed what the report would say because 12 days after the inspector's visit she had introduced a weekly examination. The results for all four classes are carefully recorded in her logbook. What persuaded her to abandon the tests we can never know, but abandon them she did very soon after the inspector, Mr Tregarthen, paid his next visit in March 1868. He repeated his criticism of the lower classes, and went on to say that "the exercises of the more advanced children are not so good as they ought to be considering the size of the school and the number of teachers employed in the instruction."

*Canon Dayman –
builder of
Shillingstone's
village school in
1854.*

Unfair, you may well think, given attendances which averaged 55 and a team of two teachers, one of whom was only 16. Perhaps Miss Bacon spent the next year teaching rather then testing but success did not come her way. The thunderclap came on 10th April 1869 when the grant was reduced by one tenth for "faults of instruction, especially in arithmetic." Maria Bacon had had lots of excuses; since 1864 she had been pleading that attendances were low because of the weather – snow and rough winds – and because the older children, especially the boys, were often needed at home. There were potatoes to be planted in March and jobs to be done in the fields and gardens in April. Haymaking took its toll in July, and the so-called harvest holiday was often not long enough for the harvest to be finished in the allotted five weeks. Then, when the gleaning was done, there was the picking of apples, acorns and potatoes.

The grant was restored to its full value in 1870, with the veiled warning that ' My Lords will expect the children at the next examination to do better in arithmetic." But poor Miss Bacon had yet more difficulties in 1871 because Elizabeth Melmoth, having passed her final examination in 1870, left Shillingstone to go to Salisbury for further training. The mistress had to cope with an average of about 60 children and, seemingly, no help until Elizabeth Brown entered the school as a paid monitor on 3rd April. Miss Bacon soldiered on until the end of 1871, averaging and recording the weekly attendances of boys and girls as well as the content of her scripture lessons, with an occasional mention of children being employed in the fields, and of minor epidemics of mumps and scarlatina. We hear no more of her.

The tone of the logbook changes with a bang on 16th January 1871: "Laura Anne Johnston took charge of this school today. Children rather noisy." By the beginning of the next week Miss Johnston was obviously having some effect because she writes: "Children not so noisy." Her section of the logbook is a joy to read, enlivened as it is by mentions of visitors – not only Canon Dayman but his wife, their daughters and their friends and, in the 1880s, Maj and Mrs Lachlan Forbes. She records lessons on a variety of subjects including map drawing, the manufacture of paper, the knitting of stockings, how to cut out a chemise, singing (lots of new songs including Twinkle, Twinkle Little Star), the rivers of England and the manufactures of England. The singing lessons were made possible because Canon Dayman had provided a harmonium, but there were days when it was needed in the church and the lessons had to be shortened or cancelled.

Miss Johnston records the punishments meted out to naughty children, mostly boys. Typical offences were stopping on the way to school to play marbles, fighting in the playground, bathing in the river, not learning home lessons, throwing stones through the lobby window, bullying a new boy, and stubbornness which earned a caning whereas repeated truancy resulted in expulsion. The apples which three boys had stolen from Mr Dominey's orchard were taken away from them and they had to write out the Eighth Commandment 50 times after school. Canon Dayman severely reprimanded boys who used bad language and others for cruelty to a flock of sheep. Six boys were kept in without dinner and had to write 60 lines for opening the door and getting into school to interrupt the girls "who were sweeping." (The inspector's report in 1875 had suggested that "the schoolroom might with advantage be kept cleaner.") The punishment for the boys who milked Mrs Ponting's cows is not revealed.

In the October of Miss Johnston's first year 46 children were absent due to measles. Just over a year later came mumps, followed in time by whooping cough, bronchitis, chickenpox, scarlatina and diphtheria – so severe a disease that it kept some children away throughout the winter. Some were ordered to stay away from school because they had caught an "infectious disease" or until they had recovered from "an eruption on their faces." Diphtheria returned early in 1883. On 4th April it claimed the life of Lydia Grace Cox who had been away from school since February. She had been admitted in September 1881 at the age of three and was the daughter of James and Louisa Cox – the eighth of their nine children. She was just over 4½ years old when she died. Their fifth child, William George, had died of "convulsions" 10 years earlier.

Miss Johnston suffered, as had Miss Bacon, from the regular absences of the older boys when they were needed for work in the gardens and fields, but attendances were also affected by bad weather. During the mid-1870s there were five unusually bad summers in a row – the rain in July 1873 was so torrential that the school could not be closed until 5pm – and there were occasions when children could not get to school because of floods, or because deep snow had made roads impassable. The school was closed in January 1879 as only three children were present, and it was closed for a week two years later. Mrs Forbes tells of skating on Benslea Pond, while potatoes were roasting on a bonfire, and of an oak tree near Hayward's bridge which had been so "cut about by the ice" that its trunk was misshapen. The river froze above the mill during these severe winters and children fortunate enough to have warm clothes and stout boots must have had a lot of fun.

During Miss Johnston's time as headmistress the school gradually became a better place in which to be taught. To begin with there was just one classroom with a gallery. In 1874 the Inspector recommended that the gallery be moved because its position meant that the teacher could not properly secure good order. Nothing seems to have been done, however. Part of the gallery floor gave way seven years later and it suffered more damage the following year. The overcrowding went on until 1877 when a new classroom was completed. It was used for the first time in May and must have been like manna from heaven – the numbers reached 100 in September that year. A stove was fitted in the classroom the following year but it was for ever smoking, sometimes so badly that the children had to be sent home. Even after the installation of a new stove in 1880 there was still trouble and the fire often had to be put out.

The classroom was made even more uncomfortable when some of the children broke the windows half way through a cold January. The police were called and the story ended at the petty sessions at Sturminster six months later, with two cautions and one fine.

The school was often ill-provisioned. The National Society provided things like desks and books but there were constant shortages of pens, paper and ink – the occasional faintness of the writing in the logbook suggests that the ink was watered down when it was running out. Mr Tregarthen had commented, in his 1877 report, on the need for a new set of maps and a school clock. The clock arrived three months later but there is no mention of the maps. Geography lessons went on apace so it must be assumed that the need was filled. There were times when the girls had to have lessons all afternoon because they had no needlework to do. One wonders whether the lessons were deemed inferior to the needlework, or vice versa. All the needlework materials seem to have been provided by Mrs Dayman who responded so promptly to news of a shortage that one suspects she had a hot line to Cherrys in Blandford. She also provided wool so that the girls could learn stocking knitting, and prizes to encourage their industry. There were four knitting prizes in 1876, going down, sixpence at a time, to a generous one shilling for the fourth.

The most obvious shortage was in teaching staff and without the help of the Dayman family it is doubtful that much learning would have gone on. There are constant references to the giving of history and reading lessons by the Rector's daughters, especially Miss Alice. Mrs Dayman would help with needlework. William Dayman would hear some reading and give the occasional magic-lantern show. Canon Dayman was the mainstay and anchor, visiting the school at least three times a week for religious instruction and examination. Maj and Mrs Forbes concerned themselves with the management of the school, with the provision of Christmas trees and with what Mrs Portman refers to as "tableaux" – she remembers being small enough to wear a white "baby frock" at her first appearance as "Little New Year" while Father Christmas gave away presents.

In September 1872 Laura Johnston's sister Janet was appointed as monitor. This must have been a comfort to the mistress because Elizabeth Brown, appointed 18 months earlier, seems often to have been absent through illness. Perhaps much of the time she was out of school was spent in private study because she was

The good old school days? Some of the pupils of yesteryear seem to be enjoying their "happiest days" more than others, and the boots tell some of the tale of tough times and poverty.

awarded a first class Queen's scholarship and apparently left the school at the end of 1875. Earlier that year Janet had become a pupil teacher and another monitor, Mary Miller, had been appointed. By the time that the Forbes family arrived in 1880 Miss Johnston had sufficient energy at the end of her school day to teach the young Florence Forbes – who counted herself lucky to have been taught by her, and only absconded once.

No details of Laura Johnston's private life appear in the logbook, nor would one expect them. But there is a hint of her departure from the school when she writes, on 13th February 1883: "The future mistress commenced work today as assistant." It is very cheering after meeting her, as it were, against the fairly humdrum background of her life at the school, to read the entry in the church register of her marriage to Walter Cox, Yeoman, on 26th June 1883. According to a paragraph in *The Western Gazette* a week later, the groom was the youngest son of Mr William Cox of Lamb House Farm, and three of the bridesmaids were sisters of the bride. The church was thronged with people, a wedding hymn was sung by the choir, a wedding march was played by Mr Loder from Okeford Fitzpaine, and showers of rice and flowers awaited the happy couple the moment they emerged from the church. After the wedding breakfast at the school house, presided over by Canon Dayman, the bride and groom left on the 2.30pm train for Southampton en route for the Isle of Wight. The numerous presents included one from the schoolchildren but it is highly improbable that any one of them enjoyed the "festivities which were kept up with great spirit until the small hours of the morning."

There are postscripts to Laura's story. It is recorded in the logbook that Mrs Cox not only gave a number of singing lessons during the next year or so but actually took over the running of the school for a week in December 1883 and again for a few days in the early part of the following year. There is no record of a handover to the new mistress but from later evidence it would appear that Laura was succeeded by her sister Janet. Laura Cox gave birth to a daughter, Alice Louise, in July 1884 and to a son, William Walter, four years later.

The logbooks make dull reading during the next 20 years or so. The frequent changes of staff may have been a talking point in the village, and the masters and mistresses may have had sparkling personalities, but the log concentrates on things like visits of local dignitaries, absences through whooping cough – it put off the visitors – influenza, mumps, ringworm, the weather and work in the fields. One of the most poignant entries, in 1891, records the absence for one week of a little girl called Louisa, and the laconic explanation that she had no boots in which to come to school.

The children attended Canon Dayman's funeral in 1890, welcomed his successor, the Rev C J Marshall, on his regular visits to the school and enjoyed a half holiday on the occasion of his daughter Ethel's wedding in 1891.

The most chaotic year in the history of the school must surely have been 1896. Mr Diprose, headmaster since October 1891, resigned in May 1896 having dutifully recorded a visit to see the managers of Corfe Mullen school and another to Sturminster "to get the school accounts audited." His headship had been good for Shillingstone. Urgent repairs had been undertaken and the inspector had declared that the school was improving despite the overcrowding – on 23rd November 1893, 113 children were present. Mr Samuel Fisher, who began his duties as headmaster on 11th May 1996, died a week later and was buried in Shillingstone on 25th May. The cause of his death is not recorded in the register. A new master, Mr Powell, took up his duties after the summer holiday and won the approval of the inspector for maintaining the efficiency of the school in elementary subjects "notwithstanding the many changes of teachers this year" – Mr Huon, the Curate, and two students from Chelsea had held the fort.

Mr and Mrs Powell – she was the sewing and infant mistress – ran the school for the next four years with the help of a succession of pupil teachers. Mr Powell was seriously concerned about extending the education of Annie Burgoyne and Florence Tooze judging by the number of entries in the logbook about their marks in examinations set by him. In one of these Florence Tooze's "answers were original and rather too independent of book knowledge"; she scored 50% so he must have been impressed by the quality of her inventive powers. He criticised their map drawing and their penmanship, ordered textbooks for their private study and allocated two half hours of study for each of them within the time-table.

He gives very full plans of work for each school year, listing the object lessons, the history and geography syllabuses, the songs and the poems to be recited. Included in the list for 1897 – admittedly for the top "standards" or classes – is Paradise Lost, Book Seven. The children would almost certainly have better understood the hockey sticks, balls and football which Mr Powell bought with some of the proceeds of a Christmas concert.

The inspector who visited the school at the end of 1897 was less concerned with the overcrowding than with the troublesome infant room chimney. It "must be attended to at once," he said, "as no fire can be got and the children are perishing with the cold." His other comments suggest a lack of pencils, of reading books for the infants and of adequate cleaning. The books were sent within weeks by the National Society and the pencils were included in a large supply of stationery received in May. There is no mention of the recommended frequent scrubbing of the toilets but, at long last, an aid grant of £15 came in November for the purchase of a new harmonium and a stove for the infants room. Suddenly, without mentioning visits to other schools or giving any other hints in the logbook, Mr Powell resigned charge of the school in April 1900. His place was taken by George Frederick Hemming who found that discipline was very bad and that manners seem to have been ignored altogether." Apparently, mental arithmetic had also been much neglected. He was soon to realise that poor attendance made it almost impossible for progress to be made and, having struggled determinedly for two years, resigned in April 1902.

His successor, William Joseph Churchill, stayed only six months – a pity, perhaps, as some of his lessons must have been fun for the children. In July he took all of them – apart from the infants and Standard I – onto the hills where they calculated the height of a tree by measuring its shadow, learned the names of the trees, saw a good example of a river basin and discovered why they "got hot when they ran." His resignation came just 10 days after notice arrived, on 20th October, of an "aid grant to provide for a necessary increase in salaries during the current year £8. Better instruction of pupil teachers, £8." There was no interregnum, so it is possible that his resignation had been expected and was not prompted by the stinginess of the award. On 3rd November 1902 the reign of Arthur Holland began – a headmaster remembered by several of his former pupils as a cruel disciplinarian.

Mr Holland was to remain head for 25 years and from the beginning, like his predecessors, he had an uphill struggle. There were more than 100 children on the register, taught in two rooms. The infants generally "moved up" to join the top division when they were seven. The older children were divided into "standards", the oldest being in Standard VII. Confusingly, there was a further division of the standards into three "classes", Class I, including Standards IV to VII, being taught by the head. Each day started with religion, from 9am until 9.45 – the Rector would join the headmaster to teach the top group and the results of the annual examination were always excellent. The rest of the day followed a scheme of work laid down by the local education committee – modern teachers would find it cramping; modern children would find it stultifying.

Each class had reading, recitation, dictation, arithmetic, history (the Tudors for Standards IV to VII; stories from reading books for the rest), geography and elementary science. The science was mostly nature study but there were object lessons on water and its uses, air, coal and the smelting of iron. There was a little singing, drawing – for boys only in the infants class – and lots of needlework for the girls. Every child had to work hard at handwriting. "Copy books" were provided for practice and it was essential to learn to write small letters "between lines" before progressing to capitals; Mr Holland's own writing is elegant and supremely legible.

Mrs Nellie Hart (née Inkpen) began school when she was only three, in 1908 – for a while she travelled there in a pushchair. She remembers being given a sand tray to play with when she was in the infants class, having a bag which hung beside her desk and held chalk and a blackboard rubber, having a much longer desk in the big room, with an inkwell in it, sitting with the girls on one side while the boys sat on the other, days when the tortoise stove worked well, and the classroom was cosily warm, and other days when it was so bitingly cold that the children had lessons wearing their outdoor coats. She also remembers needlework lessons starting off with "thimble drill" chanted with the appropriate actions:

> Here is my thimble
> High on my finger
> Like a man's hat it now stands.
> When teacher says, "One!"
> Off it must come
> And down on the desk it now stands.

The Inkpen girls wore starched pinafores to school and found their dazzling whiteness such an embarrassment that they tried to soil them on passing hedgerows as they walked. They went home each day for lunch, unlike the Gains Cross children or those who lived under the hill at White Pit, for whom it was too far to walk. Mrs Hart remembers two days' holiday for Shroton Fair, but not being allowed to go unless taken by her father. John Inkpen had served with the Gordon

Highlanders – he was a tailor and had made a coat for Lord Kitchener – and he became the village postman when he left the Army. His children would be wakened in the morning by the noise of the mail arriving in a horsedrawn trap

The school logbook reports in May 1916 that "Florence Inkpen has the measles; Reginald and Nellie are also excluded." In June so many children were ill that the school was closed. There were frequent outbreaks of sickness among the children which interrupted progress. During Mr Holland's 25 years there were no fewer than 14 closures of the school by order of the Medical Officer of Health for the county because of outbreaks of scarlet fever, whooping cough, measles, mumps, chickenpox, diphtheria and influenza – all of them serious illnesses before the advent of antibiotics. There are instances of the school being closed for only two or three weeks, but it was just as common for the epidemic to last for six weeks or more. Scarlet fever in 1903 meant no school from 27th January to 14th April, while whooping cough left classrooms empty throughout February and March in 1916. Sometimes whole families would be excluded because they lived next door to a child suffering from diphtheria, for example, or they would be sent home because they had suspected impetigo or ringworm.

The report of His Majesty's Inspector Mr Butt in 1909 admitted that "the work of the school has been hindered by the great amount of sickness which has prevailed throughout the year" and that "all things considered, the children have made very fair progress in their elementary and other subjects." The report suggests that the arithmetic should be made "as practical as possible" and that in nature lessons the children in the top class should "be encouraged to record their observations of the natural life around them." Given the number of children – there were over 100 on the register – and the conditions in which they were taught, this suggestion must have been as welcome to Mr Holland as are the demands of today's national curriculum to teachers in 2000.

Mr Butt was more openly critical of Mr Holland in 1911. While acknowledging that the children were more orderly and showed a greater interest in their lessons, the HMI went on to say that this interest might be lost if the head did not keep his marking up to date – "some of the exercises had not been corrected for a month." Although Mr Holland had obviously taken to heart the criticism in 1909 of his nature lessons – the nature lessons in 1911 were "of a practical character" – he was accused of trying "to secure too rigid a conformity" and of preventing progress in arithmetic by working all the sums on the blackboard and not allowing the children to proceed at their own pace. He seems to have spent most of his career playing catch-up.

At long last, in the reports made in 1913 by Mr Irvine and in 1914 by Mr Walsh, there was some mention of the conditions in which the children were taught. It was suggested – again – that the gallery in the infants room was inconvenient and should be removed and that "in the main room, where there are three separate classes, teaching is trying, and it is not always easy for the children to attend to what they have in hand." It is from Mr Holland, however, that we learn that there was still trouble with – you've guessed – the smoking chimney in the infants room. The children had to be sent out to play one dank November morning while the fire was put out, and the smoke was so bad in January 1917 that they had to

Classmates of 1927...

... and 1930.

be sent home. Even when it did not smoke it was so grossly inefficient that when fewer than 25% of the children made their way to school on 9th March 1917 hey had to be sent home in their wet boots because the temperature of the room was below freezing point.

Mr Holland was plagued throughout his reign by constant staff changes and the seeming impossibility of recruiting fully qualified teachers. He had to manage with a succession of pupil teachers – most of them chosen from the ranks of the paid monitors – and a succession of assistant teachers who had not been to training college. When he succeeded to the headship he inherited two pupil teachers, an assistant teacher and a paid monitor. Between them the five had charge of over 100 children. The HMI's report for the year May 1903 to May 1904 acknowledged Mr Holland's difficulties: "Considering the very weak staff the results are fairly satisfactory. Some attention should be given to the discipline"

That Mr Holland took this advice to heart is proved by the memories some of his pupils have of him. Percy Butt – no relation to Mr Butt the HMI – whose schooldays were from 1919 to 1927, cannot remember ever having been happy at school except when out of the classroom. He was in constant fear of being caned whatever he did or did not do. To be caned two or three times a day, on the hand or on the back, was quite common. Many of the boys came from very poor families and had holes in the seats of their knee-length trousers as well as in their boots. There was a "boot club" into which his mother paid a little each week so that every year she could afford the 12s 6d for a new pair of boots for him from the post office opposite the school.

Mr Butt remembers happier times helping with haymaking. The reaping was done by a horsedrawn machine but the sheaves had to be tied by hand. The children loved the ride home in the wagon. He used to earn 6d a week shaking down cider apples in the orchard behind what is now the Red House, and an old man who lived in Lanchards would give him a penny to fetch a mug of Bovril from the Rectory. The Bovril was paid for out of the poor box and on really good days he might be given an extra penny at the Rectory.

The only enjoyable part of school for Mr Butt was the gardening class. This is also possibly true of Mr Holland himself for the logbook becomes almost solely concerned with gardening classes at the beginning of 1914 – there is an almost palpable disappointment when the headmaster records that no gardening was possible because of rain. The garden was a 20-rod allotment in a field opposite the school – the war memorial was built later in the corner of the field. There was a demonstration plot and 14 small plots. The boys – gardening was only for boys – grew vegetables and fruit, and there was a prize for the tidiest garden. Percy Butt won the first prize in 1927 and went on to spend most of his working life as a gardener.

There was an important change in the staff in April 1904 when Miss Cole was replaced on her resignation by Miss Annie Burgoyne, assistant teacher, who had graduated from being a pupil teacher in 1897. The logbook mentions her quite often until 1906 when she disappears, as it were. Then, in June 1907, the log records that "Mrs Holland is unwell." The parish register of marriages resolves the mystery. Arthur Holland married Annie Stone Burgoyne in May 1907. They had no children of their own, but worked together in the school until 1927.

Little mention is made of the 1914-18 war in the logbook, apart from an entry on 1st March 1915 which blames the "Military" for leaving the school in such a condition when they used it on 27th February that the floor and desks had to be scoured before it was fit for use by the children. The cleaning operation took three days. By the winter of that year, however – possibly as a result of Lord Kitchener's "Your Country Needs You" campaign – Mr Holland became secretary to the North Dorset Recruiting Committee for the Shillingstone polling district. He was given permission by the county council and the school managers to be absent from school when necessary for this purpose and spent six half days on recruiting work before the Christmas holiday.

For many of the children the war was more damaging than all the epidemics. They lost fathers and brothers. The Inkpen family suffered grievously. Sgt Walter Inkpen was 28 when he died at Suvla Bay on 21st August 1915. Private Bertram Inkpen – a Gordon Highlander like his father – was just 18 when he was blown to pieces in France on 18th June 1916. And Sapper Ernest Inkpen, aged 21, died in Egypt from his wounds less than a month after Bert. It was a very sad childhood for Mrs Hart, her sister Florence and her brother Reg, and it must have been agonising for their parents. The Inkpens had lived next to the Burgoynes at one time and Bob Burgoyne, Mrs Holland's brother, had been a school friend of Walter – they had come up through the standards together. It was in February 1916 that Bob Burgoyne first gathered snowdrops from his garden to give to Mrs Inkpen in token of his deep sympathy. He continued to do so until her death in 1952 when they went instead to Walter's sister, Mrs Hart. The tradition has been maintained to the present day by Bob Burgoyne's daughter, Mrs Hilary Graeser, and Mrs Hart received the most recent bunch of snowdrops in January 2000.

In 1919 Mr Walsh, HMI, wrote that "since this school was reported on in 1914 no fewer than five different teachers have been in charge of the infant class and a sixth is about to be appointed. These frequent changes have retarded the progress of the infants and of the older children also." One of the teachers had not been able to control the infants, a second had not carried out suggestions made to her, and a third had had a nervous breakdown at the end of a term punctuated by frequent absences. When Miss Flora Hellier was appointed supplementary teacher in charge of the infants in March 1920 things began to improve and Mr Holland acknowledged her good work when he reported on his examination of the school in July 1921. A year later Mr Pawle, HMI, found "evidence of painstaking effort on the part of the headmaster and his staff" and praised the careful training the infants were receiving. Among the staff who had made all that effort was Miss Nellie Inkpen who had acted as paid monitress since December 1921. After his discharge from the Army in 1919 Mrs Hart's brother William went to Winchester to complete his teacher training. Mrs Hart did not follow him because her parents could not afford more fees. She worked instead at the Post Office and still remembers some of the Morse code she learned there.

Mrs Phyllis Lane (née Miller) started school in 1920. She cannot remember much about her infant days but the two or three years she spent in Mrs Holland's class were marked by the teacher's strictness, especially in needlework lessons –

knuckles would be rapped firmly if a stitch was too long. The Miller sisters went to school in knee-high lace-up or buttoned boots and pinafores, but in their eyes Mrs Holland's floor-length skirts were amusingly old-fashioned; their mother had begun to wear the shorter skirts which became fashionable in the 1920s.

Mrs Lane's family worshipped at the Methodist Chapel – the Millers were part of a large congregation which included the Rawles's, the Lewis's, the Bartletts and the Slopers. There were two Sloper families, one in Child Okeford where there was no chapel. The earlier logbooks regularly mention the absence of some children from school "to attend the Dissenters' tea party," but there are no lists to show how many on the roll were Methodists. On Monday evenings there were Band of Hope meetings in the schoolroom attached to the chapel. The Band of Hope campaigned against drinking and its battle cry was: "Lips that touch liquor shall never touch mine." There were stirring speakers like Mr Hicks of Blandford and Sammy Clark from Sturminster, but many young people went because it was a meeting place. There was also an outing to Weymouth every year, in an open-topped charabanc. Some of the hills en route were too steep for the load so some passengers had to get off and walk. The chapel was the epicentre of Mrs Lane's life and its closure was a great grief for her.

She did not grieve much when her schooldays ended although she quite enjoyed them. Mr Holland was very, very strict, she said, and even as a child she felt that "it wasn't right for the headmaster to hide his cane in the piano when the Rec or came even though Ernest Fudge and Reg Jackson were such demons." The two tearaways in question managed to sabotage the cane occasionally by cutting it so that it broke when raised.

Throughout the post-war period Mr Holland examined the whole school regularly and recorded in the logbook his satisfaction with the "very fair progress" made by the older scholars despite school closures. Mr Pawle, however, wrote after his inspection of the school in 1924 that the "reports of the work done in the periodical examinations might be more critical and helpful." But there was no hint of the bombshell that was to come three years later when he visited the school in May 1927.

The report on Mr Holland's top class was savage. "The (written) exercises need more critical revision… The children are permitted to answer indiscriminately and in chorus. They speak indistinctly and are unable to give accounts of their lessons… The older children are so ignorant of essential facts and principles and their interest (in history and geography) is so small that these subjects are of slight educational value. The poems are recited with little understanding. In arithmetic… the children are unready in dealing with simple calculations of everyday life and have not grasped the principles of the rules practised… The older children need a higher standard of effort and attainment." Mrs Holland fared better. Her lessons were "made attractive by interesting handwork illustrations." Needlework was well taught and the temporary infant teacher was "making some progress with the children whom she manages pleasantly and industriously."

Five days later the school was closed for two weeks – there was an outbreak of chickenpox – and it must have been a relief to the Hollands to have some time to themselves. The logbook does not tell us when they wrote their letters of resignation but it does include an entry written in unusually black ink and signed by Dr Cooke as chairman of the school managers:

"At a meeting of Managers held on 22 July '27 the following resolution was carried unanimously: that the meeting of Managers has received with great regret the resignation of Mr Holland, Head Teacher, and of Mrs Holland, Assistant Teacher, and desires to place on record their appreciation of their services for the period during which they have been responsible for the moral and scholastic education of the children under their care, which has met with the entire approval of the Managers."

Mr Holland's final entry in the logbook is dated 31st October 1927: "Mrs Holland is retiring from school today after 23 and a half years' service. I resign charge of this school today after 25 years' service."

In modern parlance the school would be described as "failing" and Miss Harvey – appointed to succeed – would be praised as having "turned the school around." She was a large woman – "built like an opera singer," said Leslie Bailey. And Mrs Lane, who made a nightdress for her in the needlework class, remembers that there was an awful lot of sewing to be done. Among the many awards – one of them a handbag – won by Mrs Lane for needlework was a "special prize for continued industry in needlework" awarded in September 1929 by the headmistress. Mrs Lane still has her final report, dated 25th July 1930. Her highest mark was 95 and, of course, it was for needlework.

Miss Harvey was practical in her approach. She would have read about the many and lengthy school closures and on 11th May 1928 the children were "provided with eucalyptus oil every morning after prayers and registration in the hope of preventing further absences for coughs and colds." There were to be absences, but there seem to have been only two closures – one because of a scarlet fever epidemic and the second because of an outbreak of mumps. Miss Harvey did not necessarily have a rest though. During the second closure, in February 1936, she and her assistant were seconded to the village school at Bishop's Caundle as the two teachers there were absent.

Mr Charlie Stride gave swimming lessons for the schoolchildren – his pupil in this case is Raymond Snook.

There were also days when the children stayed away because of heavy snow or severe flooding. But at least one family showed real determination. The Peacocks lived in a cottage right up the drove at Beremarsh, according to Mrs Graeser, and when the river flooded the youngest child, a girl of eight or nine, would be rowed by her 16-year-old brother from their cottage up to the main road. All the children thought it was wonderful to come to school by boat.

On the same day as Miss Harvey administered the eucalyptus oil she caned a boy for stealing and lying, and did it in front of all the upper division "in order to put an end to the pilfering which has been troubling the school for several weeks.' Nor was she less than firm with grown-ups. A grandmother who used abusive language when she complained that her grandson had been punished undeservedly "was asked to go, or be reported to the managers and the education committee." She very quickly went.

During Miss Harvey's headship there is evidence of the growing interest of the Government in children's health. The "nit nurse" visited regularly to make sure their heads were free of lice and, in Shillingstone, they almost always were. Dentists visited, and it is recorded that in 1929 a dentist "removed the teeth of 10 children" – obviously not to be taken literally. The makers of toothpaste soon joined the act and in November 1932 the Ivory Castle League was formed with the help of Gibbs Dentifrice, who produced a lantern lecture on the care of the teeth which Miss Harvey showed to the children. In 1943 the Rector's daughter presented badges to 24 children who had brushed their teeth twice daily for 12 weeks – these little defenders of "ivory castles" were called "Crusaders" – and later that year the High Commissioner for New Zealand presented more badges and bars. Miss Harvey got two for the price of one on that occasion for he also gave a talk on New Zealand. The campaign was still being fought the following year when 16 children were presented with gold stars for completing three periods of 12 weeks' teeth cleaning.

On 29th June 1931 it is recorded in the logbook that 10 boys left the school at 3.30 pm for a swimming lesson given by Mr C R Stride, a member of the Education Committee. Three days later there was a lesson for 10 girls – Mr Stride had promised to give instruction in swimming throughout the summer term. He had been "a photographer and maybe a correspondent in the Boer War, and used to take school and village photographs using a big camera on a tripod and disappear under a black cloth," says Mrs Tricia Cooper (née Sloper). The group would walk down Hine Town Lane, past Mr Stride's garden at Broadclose, past the recreation ground, along the main road to Townsend, down Holloway Lane and across a field to the river where there was easy access to a natural pool. Mrs Cooper remembers how impatient they were to get into the water after such a long walk.

But the swimming lessons equipped the children to have fun in the river, as confirmed by the happy memories of Mrs Christine Pope (née Bartlett) and Mrs Irene Haines (née Bastable), who both recall spending warm summer days down at what was called "the bathing isle" near the station. There was a diving board and steps for the more timorous. They would sometimes take packed lunches, or time their departure for home by the arrival of the 12.55 train.

The first group of girls to have a swimming lesson were accompanied by Miss Doreen Stokes who had come from Deri, South Wales, at the beginning of the term to teach Standards II and III. It was an appointment which would truly benefit the village. In August 1935 Miss Stokes married Reginald Sloper and went to live at 27 Church Road. Her daughter, Tricia, says that "married women teachers were not allowed, but she continued at the school for another term because no one was available to fill the post." She suggested her cousin for the task and in January 1936 Miss Myra Jones arrived from South Wales. Mrs Sloper remained involved with the school and was one of its managers for a while. She became clerk to the parish council in 1954, a position which she held for 42 years. She was awarded an MBE in 1994 and the citation speaks of the many hours of unstinting service she gave for no more than token financial recompense.

During a seven-month absence of Miss Harvey, to do voluntary work in British Columbia, Miss Treneman took charge of the school. She is described in the HMI's report as an experienced supply mistress and she certainly made herself liked. Mrs Graeser says that each day ended with a few chapters of a very exciting story and, to ensure the children's good behaviour, Miss Treneman only had to suggest that naughtiness would result in there being no story.

The logbook records the visits of several HMIs – including Mr Pawle – during the first few years of Miss Harvey's headship. They obviously went away satisfied and there was no full-scale inspection until the summer of 1930. Mr Pawle's report must have pleased everyone connected with the school. The headmistress had done a great deal to remedy the defects set out in the last report. The details of the curriculum had been thoughtfully planned. The work of the staff and children was reviewed critically. The written exercises reached a better standard, especially in the junior group. The children displayed a keener interest in all their lessons and the tone of the school had much improved. There was even praise for the managers whose practical interest in the welfare of the school "contributes in no small way to its general efficiency."

According to the managers' minutes, they were at that time Dr Cooke (chairman), Mrs Kyrle Chapman, Mrs Webber, Mr Tate, Mr Cox and Mr Melmoth.

Miss Harvey, who left Shillingstone in October 1937, was commended by an HMI's report in January of that year for her very good influence on the children "by reason of her high ideals." She had broadened their horizons, literally, by taking them on "educational journeys" – one to Milton Abbey, Wareham, Corfe Castle, Studland, Poole and Wimborne, and another to the Rufus Stone, Southampton docks to see the Empress of Britain, and on to Salisbury. She also opened up the school to parents as well as to friends and managers, and the annual prize days began to include exhibitions of needlework and woodwork as well as displays of the children's work in all subjects.

There is no direct mention in the logbook of the threat of another world war, but the school had a holiday on 25th November 1938 to enable all the staff to attend a course of ARP (Air Raid Precautions) lectures in Blandford, and the children must have been aware of the looming crisis. When war did break out, schools were closed throughout the next week. Shillingstone reopened on 12th September with the same number of children – there were about 60 on roll – and it seems that practical woodwork and cookery classes were the only casualties at this stage.

On 17th June 1940 the war was suddenly brought closer by the arrival of 36 London children in charge of two male teachers. The evacuees were aged from four to 14 and were initially absorbed into the school. The Methodist schoolroom was borrowed to make more space and the senior class was taught there by Mr Pomroy, one of the London teachers. It soon became obvious that it would be too costly to provide sufficient toilets at the schoolroom and within a month, and after visits by two London County Council inspectors, the top class was moved back into the main school building. It had been discovered that its official capacity was 120 children, but imagine the crowding.

During the first part of the summer holiday in 1940 – it was split during the war, with two weeks in August and a further week or two in October or November – trenches were dug in the field behind the school for the children to use during air raids. Mrs Haines has vivid memories of being shepherded down into them – they were deep and often muddy – with a gasmask slung over her shoulder. The logbook records a number of alerts in the spring of 1941, one of them lasting for two hours which cannot have been any fun. One afternoon they were in the trenches as planes passed over. They were told not to look up but Miss Jones did. "It was a wonderful sight," she said, "because they looked like silver birds in formation, shining in the sun."

The school once again needed to be reformed in 1942 and the person chosen to do so this time was Miss Meadway. She was a disciplinarian, according to Fred Savory who later became one of her most devoted admirers. When he left school at 14 she said sadly: "Well, Savory, you won't learn, you won't study, you just fool around." But when he went to see her six months later, having realised just what a fool he had been, she unstintingly gave him help and advice. "Go and join the library," she said, "and pick up the first three novels you see. Read them, and when you've read them borrow three more. You will broaden your outlook and be able to make better conversation."

She was very strict, Mrs Cooper confirmed, "and we were all a bit frightened of her." Some mothers were in awe of her, too. Sometimes boys were caned, but never girls. Lesser punishments for both sexes were a slap on a bare arm or having to stand at the front of the class with hands on head. There was strict silence while the headmistress sat on her stool at a high wooden desk and the children queued to have their arithmetic checked. There was chanting of tables, learning of them and testing on them – the children were afraid not to know them for fear of being kept in. The maths teacher at Blandford Grammar School commented that all children coming from Shillingstone always knew their multiplication tables – and a growing number of children won scholarships to the grammar school.

There was some fun to be had, too, however. Miss Jones remembers the day when Miss Meadway decided to take gym classes herself and appeared as a vision in brown, dressed in a short, above-the-knee brown gymslip, brown blouse and brown stockings and plimsolls. The logbook records that school closed at 3.30pm one Friday so that Miss Meadway and Miss Jones might take the junior and senior classes on a blackberry-picking expedition "to assist the Government's Food Production Scheme." Mr Stride continued with his swimming lessons. The county council provided apparatus for football, tennis and rounders, as well as some plimsolls. And in 1942 school life was transformed by the installation of electricity and the asphalting of the playground.

A contribution of £5 was made to the cost of the playground improvements by the Shillingstone Social Committee which ran the Village Hut. The committee's minute book for 1942 also mentions a Christmas party for all the schoolchildren – 24 prizes at a shilling each were bought for competitions and games, and at the close of the party the children were given 1s saving stamps on a card. The real highlight, though, must have been the buns and cakes "instead of the usual bread and butter," and the film show presented by Mr Bailey.

At a time when the nation was being urged to "Dig for victory" gardening tools were provided for the girls and some children obtained exemption from school for the three days before the second tranche of the summer holidays, and throughout October, to help with potato picking during the wartime shortage of men. Mrs Haines enjoyed it enormously. She admits that she would have used any excuse to get out of school, but there was a double bonus in the shape of cash payments. She had never been so rich in her life. The children took packed lunches, the farmer at Gains Cross was very kind, and it was sunny and warm that autumn.

By contrast, winters in school were still cold – Mrs Cooper suffered chilblains on her toes for years and the children who wanted warm milk at playtime had it heated in a crate on top of the stove. The milk came from Pope's Farm at Hillsfoot where there was a Jersey herd. It was very creamy and sometimes smelled of hay. It came in little bottles and the cardboard top had a hole in the middle which made them useful for craft lessons, especially for making pom-poms.

In April 1943 Miss Meadway raised £8 15s 6d by holding a school concert at the Hut, and by August that year she had received enough money from donations to be able to spend £11 10s 11d on a Murphy wireless set. County paid 15s for the plug. The logbook does not reveal when or how the radio was used, but Mrs Cooper and her contemporaries made scrapbooks of the progress of the Allies in Europe in the latter stages of the war, so they probably listened to news bulletins. They were certainly made aware of the end of the war in Europe because there was a two-day holiday. The downside of the war's end was that the cooked dinners which had been supplied since September 1943 from Okeford Fitzpaine's communal kitchen, at a cost of 5d a day, were cancelled for a while on 23rd May as the voluntary car pool service ended.

Changes in school life after the war included the demise of gardening classes when the allotment land on Poplar Hill was sold for housing development. And one fact not recorded in the school log is that in 1946 Miss Meadway was the first woman to be elected to the parish council. She went on to become its chairman in 1953. Mr Savory says it was she who named Wessex Avenue.

She also formed the school's parent teacher association in 1951. Parents had become increasingly involved with the school during Miss Harvey's headship, almost certainly because of her active encouragement of their presence at prizegiving – she had begun to call it Parents Day in 1937.

In the absence of former benefactors like Mrs Forbes, Mrs Chapman and Mrs

Maypole dancing in the school playground in the 1950s.

Webber – many people in the village called them "the toffs" – Miss Meadway turned to fundraising on the children's behalf. In December 1948 every child in the school took part in a concert given at the Hut in aid of the Christmas party fund for all the children of the village. The school drama fund was the beneficiary of the following winter's fundraising event. And by December 1950 the school had a treasurer who took charge of the money collected after a nativity play performed in the church. In July 1951 there was an entertainment on the Rectory lawn which included maypole dances, revived after a lapse of many years. The guest speaker was Mrs Torkington from Croft House School who spoke to parents of the necessary link between them and school in the education of their children.

Village schoolchildren in the 1950s... And (opposite page) a class of '89. Picture by Helmut Eckardt.

The next logical step – Miss Meadway had perhaps primed Mrs Torkington to sow the seed – was to involve the parents more actively and, in September 1951, a meeting was held with the object of forming the school's PTA. It soon got to work, providing a Christmas party with a tree, giving a challenge cup to be presented at the Three Okefords school sports, and providing some of the prizes

which Mrs Portman distributed at the end of the following summer, with her usual prizes for wildflower collections. "The toffs" were almost no more, and from now on self-help was to be the order of the day.

Like all village schools during the second half of the 20th century, Shillingstone's continued to evolve and grow in stature and educational achievement, if not necessarily in numbers on roll, meeting all the challenges and changes ordained by successive national Governments. Unlike too many other village schools, Shillingstone's has not closed. Far from it. After some worrying times in the late 1970s and early 80s it is thriving and has entered the new millennium as strong as ever. Indeed, it can lay claim now to being one of the last remaining truly village schools in Dorset – essentially having just the parish of Shillingstone as its catchment area, although a number of parents from outside the village also choose it because of its excellent reputation.

That might perhaps not have been the case had it undergone the major change first intended for it in the wake of the 1944 Education Act, and reconsidered in 1968. Plans were drawn up, in accord with the 1944 Act, for a new "area school" in Shillingstone to serve the Three Okefords. This scheme was abandoned after taking into account the views from the three villages. Plans in 1960 for a new two-class school just for Shillingstone were a victim of the country's economic crisis at that time, and in 1966 the county education authority decided to revert to the original plan. Three sites were looked at – a field beside Hine Town Lane, the field at Pepper Hill next to Everetts Lane and land at Townsend next to the allotments. Then Child Okeford entered the bidding with a potential site for the new "area school" in that village. Over the next three years the Shillingstone school managers pursued vigorously their case for the new school, culminating in a public meeting in the Portman Hall on Monday 21st July 1969 attended by the school managers, 73 villagers and three "observers" from Child Okeford. A number of people felt each village should keep its own school, and it was eventually resolved unanimously:

"That by every effort and by all means a school should be built in Shillingstone for Shillingstone children and all who wish to come to it."

To pursue this aim, an action committee was formed, but to no avail and the village's hopes just faded away.

The proponents of area schools returned with a vengeance, however, in the late 1970s and early 80s, this time backed by the preparation of Dorset County Council's first Structure Plan and an onslaught on village schools across the whole country. To counter this threat, and with the outspoken backing of headteacher Mrs Kate Ashcroft, another Action Committee was formed, this time with a view to adding an extra classroom to the existing school – an aim that was quite strongly opposed initially by both diocesan and county education officers. They warned that any new building, even a temporary one, would immediately become the property of either the church or the county while the school governors, as they had by then become, would have to bear the full cost of cleaning and maintaining it. Fundraising went ahead nevertheless, and on Thursday 27th September 1984 the Bishop of Sherborne, the Rt Rev John Kirkham, dedicated the new classroom. Housing development in the village brought increasing numbers of children to the school, vindicating the action taken, and in 1990 the new building was doubled in size with the blessing of the diocese. The following year the county council agreed to take over responsibility for what they had derisorily called when it first went up "the governors' hut."

Further major change came with the decision in 1996 that the school, by then under the leadership of headteacher Mr Brian South and chairman of governors the Rev Michael Turner, should go Grant Maintained, while remaining a Church of England school. The new status, which was being encouraged nationally by the Conservative Government of the day, gave the school almost total independence as well as considerable extra funding. That made possible the replacement of both the "governors' hut" and the other much older "temporary" classroom with two much larger rooms in a semi-permanent building that also provided a new kitchen. GM status turned out to be shortlived when Labour won the 1997 general election and set about returning such schools to the maintained sector. So Shillingstone once again became a Voluntary Aided church school.

Now, at the beginning of the 21st century all three Okeford primary schools are bursting at the seams, and there is a clear preference for educating young children, wherever possible, within their own communities. Shillingstone school has served its community pretty well for 146 years – albeit with successive heating devices remaining a perennial problem right up to the present day. As the school moves towards its 150th anniversary there are once again plans afoot to relocate it to the other end of the village. This time, will those plans materialise? And how will the school continue to fare over the next century and a half? All those who know it must surely give it high marks and wish it well.

As the Ofsted report of June 1998 commented: "The caring environment with a positive Christian ethos and the very good relationships within the school contribute significantly to the pupils' good attitudes to learning and their very good behaviour."

The Children's Viewpoint

In the final year of the 20th century the children of class three at Shillingstone CE VA Primary School put together their thoughts on what the school was like in 1999. There is much in their comments which will strike a familiar chord with those who were on the roll 50 years ago and no doubt will ring true for those attending in 50 years' time. As always, the school was on the point of change, in this case preparing for Information and Communication Technology to make its impact on the way in which children learn. Already computers and CD Roms were in general use but the school now had an internal network installed and within the next 12 months all the classrooms were due to be linked to the World Wide Web. How wonderful and amazing it would have seemed to those who attended 50 years ago and how quaint and archaic it will be to those who read this in 50 years' time...

Most people in the village walk to school but some come by car and people from different villages have to come by car. We arrive at school at about quarter to nine and Mrs Antell, the lollypop lady, stops the traffic so that we can cross the road. You go into school through a little gate and cross the playground. When we come into school we put our coats and bags on our pegs in the cloakroom and go to our classroom. It is very crowded in school in the morning because all the mothers of the infants bring them and sometimes they bring babies in prams. When it rains everyone is inside and it is impossible to move.

School starts at nine o'clock so you have to be there at five to nine but we have to be sitting in our places reading quietly. In the top class we go straight to the library area and choose a reading book. We have reading groups and each day one has to read to Mr South or Mrs Phillips. They sit in a group with a set of books and everyone takes turns to read. We have books by people like Roald Dahl, Phillipa Pearce and lots of others that we enjoy reading.

After reading we usually have English which lasts until we go for assembly. After assembly we go out to play for 15 minutes. The top class has the front playground and the middle class the back playground. The infants have a separate playtime which is just as well because the older boys play football which is really dangerous. When the bell goes we all line up and then go back into school for the next lesson which is usually maths and lasts right up to lunchtime which is at 12.15. When it is lunchtime we clear everything off the desks, sit in our places and say grace. Then we go to the cloakroom and get out our lunchboxes. Everyone stays for lunch and brings a packed lunch and most people have sandwiches, crisps and yoghurt or fruit or chocolate bars. Classes one and two have dinner ladies but in class three the people on each table take it in turns to tidy the table. When all the tables are cleared we go out to play until the bell goes at one o'clock and we come in for afternoon school.

During the afternoon we do all the other things we have to do in school like science, history and art. The children in the other classes have a playtime in the middle of the afternoon but in the top class we do not stop until school ends at 3.15. At home time we clear all our things away and say a prayer and go home. Most of the children in class three walk home on their own but the younger children are met by their parents who wait in the playground for them. On a Tuesday there are after-school activities and we have football and netball or in the summer there is athletics which last until about quarter past four. In the top class we usually have homework to take home and bring back the next day.

If you look round the school you will see that at the front we have a playground with a high wire fence which is supposed to stop our balls going into the road but quite often we kick them over and they get burst by a lorry. There is a narrow channel to connect to the back playground which is very long and thin with the shed for PE things at the end. At one side of the playground is the high fence but on the other side is a big hawthorn hedge and our balls often get stuck on it and we have to get a broom to get them down. On both playgrounds there are lines, hopscotch and posts for netball. There is also a bench to sit on which was dedicated by the year six when they left in 1998. At the side of the school is a drinking fountain that does not work very well and often gets blocked up. Near it up high on the school wall is a big green and white sign from the old railway station which says "SHILLINGSTONE."

We all like the playground because it is a fun place to run about but in the summer the tarmac gets very hot and we use the field for playtimes. The field is quite big and it has a football pitch marked on it and two goals so that we can play football. There is also a long jump pit which we use when we do athletics. In the summer we have a running track marked on the field so that we can have a sports day. There is also a climbing frame but we are not allowed to use it because

Mike Morris's sketch of the oldest parts of the school, with the old railway station sign on the side wall.

it is on the hard ground and does not have a soft landing mat. Across the field is a path which leads to a little gate into the churchyard which we go along when we go to church for assembly. There is a wire fence between the field and the churchyard and quite often there is a funeral in the churchyard and we watch the men digging the grave with a digger.

The school has a conservation area in one corner of the playing field. It was built for the school in 1994 to help the children learn about wildlife. The pond is home to many creatures such as frogs, tadpoles, newts, dragonflies, waterboatmen and snails. We use the pond for looking at wildlife close-up and can catch things and look at them with a magnifying glass. The infants go there mostly to look at the tadpoles. In summer, grass and flowers cover most of the area and there are lots of stinging nettles which are good for caterpillars. Around the area is a big hedge which consists of hawthorn, privet, dogrose, blackthorn and lots of other trees. One of the parents looks after the conservation area and has to cut the grass and nettles and clean the weed and fungi from the pond so that the wildlife has room to roam.

When you go into the school you go in through a door next to the two new classrooms and the entrance is not very big. There are several big noticeboards which have things like notices for parents or work which the children have done. Right in front of you is a gap in the wall which goes to the cloakroom and this is not very big either. There are more than 80 pegs for our coats and bags but not very much room so we cannot all go in at once and things get pushed off the pegs.

There is a sign with an arrow which says "office" and if you follow it you will come to the school office. It is quite a small room but full of all kinds of equipment which people use for their work. Along two of the walls are long desks where Mr South and the secretary can work. Under them are lots of cupboards and drawers and a big iron safe to keep the money in. On the walls are some shelves which are covered with files. The secretary is Mrs Stickland and she works in the office most of the time. She has lots of files with all the papers about the school in them and she has equipment like the photocopier, computer and the fax to help her. She has lots of different things to do because she looks after all the money for swimming and the PTA, any fundraising and also all the money the school gets from the Government. In 1998 the school spent over £300,000 which was a lot of money to look after. She has to look after all the mail and answer letters and order all the books and equipment that the school needs.

From the school entrance you can go straight into the hall and this is the biggest room in the school but it is not big enough for the older children to do PE properly. The green floor is made of a rubbery material, and in the corner is a big pile of mats and benches for PE. There is a climbing frame which swings out from the wall and some ropes on another frame can also be swung out. In another corner is the piano and there is a music trolley with lots of instruments and music stands. The walls have lots of big noticeboards covered with children's work. Doors out of the hall lead to the lower juniors' classroom, to the "little room" and to the front porch which is now a storeroom. Along one side of the hall are three arched windows with blinds which can be pulled down when we watch television.

We use the hall for assemblies, music, special workshops, dance and drama, and the infants use it for PE.

What we call the "little room" is very small and has no windows, just a skylight. It was the coke store when the school had coal fires. Later it became the office but it was too small and when the new office was built it became a staffroom. About a week later it became a "special needs" room! Now it is used for the reception children as well as for special needs. It contains a great deal of equipment. The reception children use the games, toys, number lines and alphabets. Other things in there are for the teachers' use like reference books, videos, catalogues, a comb binder and a laminator. On one wall is a huge picture of two cupids and on another is the control panel for the burglar alarm. It is only a very small room but it is used all the time by groups as a place to work.

The school has three main classrooms, two of which are very new and one is very old and quite small. There are about 24 children in class two, which uses this smaller room, and their teacher is Mrs Exley who also takes netball and athletics and is good at teaching drama and dance. The old kitchen next door to Mrs Exley's classroom is no longer used as a kitchen, but as a store cupboard. There are three computers for the pupils in Mrs Exley's class, and two trolleys hold the class library.

The two new classrooms were built in 1998. The teacher of the infants class, which has 32 children, is Mrs Murch. She is helped by Mrs Whitfeld, and Mrs Long who works with the reception children. Mrs Murch also teaches music – everyone learns to play the recorder. In one corner of this classroom is a playhouse. In another corner is the reading area. A sink and wet area has places for children to do their painting. The classroom has three computers and it is a bright and colourful room with lots of pictures and paintings on the walls.

Next to the infants classroom is the new kitchen where once a week Mrs Watts teaches cooking which is really good fun. We make things like lemon meringue pie and pizza which we can take home. In the kitchen are two sinks, each with hot and cold taps, and a fridge to keep food in. An oven is set into the work surface. Because the kitchen does not have any windows it gets very hot so it has a fan in the ceiling.

In class three there are 27 of us. The teacher is Mr South who is also headteacher. He is helped by Mrs Phillips, the classroom assistant. On Thursdays the class is taught by Mrs Horder so that Mr South can work in the office. Like the other new classroom ours has big windows which look across to the church, and beyond to Shaftesbury and to Duncliffe Wood near Gillingham. On a very clear day you can even see King Alfred's Tower which is near Wincanton. In one corner of our room we have the school library so we do not have to walk far if we want a book. Our desks are arranged in four big rectangles made by putting four or five of them together. In the middle of each is a tray to hold scissors, rulers and pots for coloured pencils and felt-tip pens. At the side of the room there are cupboards in which we each have a tray for our own things. We have three computers in the classroom, all of them fairly new. One came from Tesco because everyone collected vouchers when they went shopping. On the walls of the classroom are noticeboards on which our work is pinned, and at the front is a blackboard for the teacher to use. Three radiators make the room nice and warm in the winter and high up on the wall is a burglar alarm sensor which can pick up heat and movement to set off the alarm if anyone walked in at night. We think the classroom is just about the right size, and much better than the old one which was very crowded and got very cold in the winter.

In our maths lessons we learn about things like angles, time, fractions, decimals, grid references, temperature, percentages and negative numbers. We learn to measure weight in grams and kilograms; length in centimetres, metres and kilometres; volume in cubic centimetres; temperature in degrees Celsius; capacity in litres; and angles in degrees. On the computer we use Logo to learn about degrees and angles. In Logo there is a little turtle on the screen which you can send in all directions when you type instructions into the computer. We learn how to use mathematical symbols instead of words and we use maths all the time even when playing games, or in shops, or in sport to measure how far someone has jumped. We do lots of mental arithmetic and some of us can work out big sums very quickly in our heads.

In English we learn how to write and about different kinds of writing and different authors. We learn about things like punctuation, direct speech and contractions. On the computers we use a desktop publishing programme called Ovation. Sometimes we have used it to make pages for newspapers. We have also used the computers for play scripts which we can print out to give everyone a copy. As well as writing we read a lot and have to do things like comprehension and book reviews. Sometimes authors have come to school and told us about how they write their books. Most people in the class like reading and we are good at reading.

In science we learn about things like how the human body works and how plants grow. We do topics like the Earth in space and learn about the solar system and the planets. We sometimes do experiments to find things out, like how good materials are for insulating a container of hot water. Sometimes we make things like pinhole cameras or colour wheels. We grow peas and beans in plastic bottles so that we can watch them and record what happens.

Technology is another interesting subject because we have to design and make all sorts of things like buggies which have electric motors powered by batteries. We have got electric shaper saws, drills and hot glue guns so that we can cut up and join pieces of wood to make a chassis and fix on wheels and axles. When we do technology we have to work in groups and then test what we have made to see if we have been successful.

In history at the moment our topic is Invaders and Settlers which is about the Celts, Romans, Saxons and Vikings and how they invaded Britain and took over control. We have also had topics about the Aztecs, the Victorians and the Greeks. When we did the Greeks we had a drama workshop and made up a play about them which we wrote on the computer and then acted.

One of our best subjects is art and we really enjoy doing lots of different things with different materials. For painting we have a flat white palette each and a lot of different sizes of brushes and a variety of colours which we mix to make other shades. We have done things like shades of colour patterns, pictures from the

Greek myths, self-portraits, landscapes from the classroom window, and the Iron Man. We use clay to make models of spacemen, nativity figures, models of animals and all kinds of things of our own choice. We have put clay on wire shapes and we have made action figures out of wire. This year we had an artist in residence who helped us make a giant willow withy sculpture of the Iron Man which was so huge we had to take it apart to get it outside. Pencil and paper drawing is one of the simplest things we do but we also use charcoal and chalk which are good to smudge and blend colours but it smudges very easily so you have to be careful not to get your clothes in it. Pastels are great but the downside is that you get your fingers very messy. When we do print making we are only allowed one or two bits of polystyrene because it is very expensive. You make an indent in the polystyrene using a blunt pencil, not pressing too hard so as not to pierce the polystyrene. Then you put ink on using a roller, being careful not to press too hard. Finally you place the polystyrene on a piece of paper and roll it very firmly with a clean dry roller. Another thing we do is marbling. We have a half-filled tray of water and special inks which we drip into the water. We mix different coloured inks and when we get a pattern we like, we slide a piece of paper into the tray. When you take it out you have a lovely marble-effect pattern.

We enjoy music and do lots of it. Everybody learns to play the recorder starting in reception and taught by Mrs Murch. We have different groups according to ability, and we have three different kinds of recorder – the smallest is the descant, the next is a treble and the biggest is a tenor. The top two groups go to a music festival in Salisbury every year. We learn one or two pieces and compete against other groups of the same age, and we have been awarded first, second and third place certificates. We do lots of singing and Mrs Murch teaches us Christmas, Easter and end-of-term songs. Sometimes one of us gets chosen to sing a solo. We have two or three concerts or performances each year to which our parents are invited. These include nativity plays and shows like Oliver, Cinderella, Puss in Boots, and Joseph and the Amazing Technicolor Dreamcoat which we have done in the village hall. Mrs Laws, the church organist, accompanies us on the piano, Mrs Paulley helps with the costumes and Mrs Exley helps us learn to act. We have lots of percussion instruments which we use for concerts and productions, and sometimes we are visited by a musician who gives us a music workshop where we make up our own pieces of music using the percussion instruments. Recently Andy Baker from the Bournemouth orchestra brought his double bass which would hardly fit in the hall and played some pieces such as the Jaws theme. He also brought a didgerydoo and a trumpet which we tried to play unsuccessfully. Last year we were invited to the Blast from the Proms concert at Poole Arts Centre. We all made top hats out of cardboard but when we got there we were the only ones wearing them. However, everyone in the audience had Union Jacks to wave. We sang along to Land of Hope and Glory which was strengthened by the orchestra and someone hitting an enormous gong. In the 1812 Overture they fired fake cannons which shot out smoke and made a loud bang. Finally, a woman in a Union Jack dress sang Rule Britannia in opera style.

Every day in school we have a Christian assembly. As we walk in the teacher lights a candle which means it is assembly time. Sometimes we have stories read to us, sometimes from the Bible about Jesus or the feeding of the 5,000 or one of the many other stories. After that we sing a hymn while four or five people play the music on the recorder. At the end of assembly we have a prayer and a quiet time to think. Every Monday we have a service with the Rector in church. As well as singing hymns we talk about a lot of different things. But best of all in every assembly Mr Turner pulls out something from his pockets to help him tell the story. Among other things he has produced a kettle, a kite, a huge cross, a sword, a pot plant, but most amazing of all was a parasol. But that is not the only reason we like him, he is very funny as well. We think we are very lucky to have Mr Turner as our Rector. Every year we have a harvest festival. The little children take decorated boxes full of fruit and vegetables to be sold at the Harvest Supper. The older children take useful things to help children in schools and hospitals in poorer countries, and usually we learn about the people we help. Also we have services at Easter and at Christmas. At the end of the school year we have a leavers service where we always sing The Journey of Life and One More Step Along the Way. The Rector gives each leaver a Bible and the leavers give a present to the school.

Sport is great. We all enjoy it and do lots of different things during the year and most of the boys are mad about football. Our team participates in cups and tournaments and has always been pretty good. In the past we have won the North Dorset tournament and we usually come very close to winning. We have recently received a new kit and it makes us look really professional. Our colour is blue all over with white stripes round the tops of the socks. We get lots of extra training from other clubs around Dorset. Of course most of the girls have got a favourite sport too and that is netball, and they often play against other schools and take part in tournaments. Because most of the girls like netball the training has to be split into two different days with Mrs Exley who trains them. During the summer we train for athletics and take part in the area sports. We also have our own sports day when the teachers divide the school into various teams so that each has a mix of year groups. The one or two year six children in each team are captains and they help and encourage the younger children. The teams are named after events like the world cup or themes like fruit or animals – for instance, Mighty Mangoes, Dynamite Dragonflies and Leaping Lions. The teams compete against each other in various events such as long jump, skipping, shuttle relay and obstacle races. Every Thursday in the winter when it is too cold to go outside the school hires a double-decker bus to take us to Bryanston School where we have swimming lessons. By the end of year six everyone is confident in the water and can swim a long distance in several strokes. Once a year a fun gala takes place in which everyone who goes swimming takes part. We race against each other in whichever stroke we choose. Even the youngest children have their own races which are usually a width using armbands or floats. Another annual swimming event is a Swimarathon at Clayesmore Sports Centre. This is a charity event where the strongest swimmers in the school collect sponsors for an hour long non-stop relay. The money we raise is donated to a charity of our own choice.

As well as work we do lots of things in school which are fun. Most Fridays we have Golden Time which is a reward for good behaviour and work during the past week. During Golden Time we can choose from a selection of activities such as board and table and construction games, arts and crafts, use of computers, or quiet reading or writing. We sometimes have fun raising money for good causes with things like a bad hair day or a non-uniform day when people pay to dress up or to come in with amazing things done to their hair – and even the teachers take part. In the autumn term the year six children always organise a sale for the Children in Need charity. It is good fun to organise and raises over £100. At Christmas we have a party in the hall when the PTA gives us a Christmas lunch and we have Christmas pudding which we made with Mrs Watts and lots of jelly and ice-cream. On the last afternoon of the autumn term Father Christmas comes and gives everyone a present. In the summer the year sixes go to Weymouth for a week and stay in a hostel with children from the other three schools in our cluster. Each day they go to Weymouth Outdoor Activity Centre to do things like climbing, caving, canoeing and sailing. It is brilliant because we cannot normally do these things and also we get to meet other children who will be going on to Sturminster Newton High School with us. At the end of the school year in the summer term we have a games evening when the children have a big game of rounders with the parents and past pupils. There are also races like sack races and slow bicycle races and after that we have egg throwing. Everyone buys an egg and lines up with a partner. You have to throw the egg to your partner but when you have thrown it you have to move another step apart and throw again. When the eggs break you get covered in egg so it is best when you watch other people.

* We would like this to be a sort of time capsule to tell people in the future what it was like being at Shillingstone School in 1999. The school has changed a lot even while we have been here and we think that it will change again in the future.

The Shillingstone schoolchildren of 2000 with their teachers. Picture by Michael Head.

Croft House School 1941-1997

One day in 1941 a visitor staying with Lt-Col and Mrs Oliver Torkington expressed the opinion that any great project needed more careful planning and forethought, and could not be accomplished overnight. The following morning Esther Torkington came down to breakfast and announced that she was going to start a school. Thus Croft House School was born. For over half a century it filled a very particular gap in the world of education, as well as providing much employment in Shillingstone.

The start in the Torkingtons' own home, to provide education for their daughter and the daughters of friends, established the tradition of family feeling and concern which were hallmarks of the school. Individual care was at the heart of Croft's philosophy and, in a disciplined family environment, each girl was encouraged to fulfil her own potential which for some was academic success for others achievement in artistic, athletic or practical areas. Under the guidance of Caesar and Pop, as the founders were affectionately known, the school grew rapidly from small beginnings and by the end of the first year numbers had outgrown Croft House and annexes had opened at the Rectory, Cross House and Burlton Lodge… and still it grew.

In Mrs Torkington's review of the first 10 years she writes of the work achieved in art, music, drama, games and riding, and throughout Croft's history these were to be the salient features of the school.

Soon Grange, built by Mrs Kyrle Chapman in 1904, was purchased with its chapel, walled garden and tennis courts and in 1947 Manor Farm was obtained for the junior boarders (boys as well as girls). The same year the old gymnasium was built with its stage and green room. Even in the 1950s all the school walked up

Leisure time in the Blue Room at Croft with headmistress Mrs Esther (Caesar) Torkington.

through the village to share all meals with the headmistress. Mrs Rosina Newman, who was under-cook at Croft and who lived at Grange Cottage, tells the story of the girls complaining that when they walked past her home they were greeted by loud wolf whistles. This very nearly caused trouble for Mr Newman until it was revealed that the Newmans' budgerigar was the culprit.

Numbers continued to rise. Cottages and buildings, in the village and further afield, were used for the growing number of boarders. A swimming pool was built on the Croft site, while at Grange a sports field, a cross-country course and a

Croft House (above) ... and Grange.

125

gymkhana field enlarged the scope of games and riding. In the latter, Croft became a force to be reckoned with, being probably the first school in the country to boast an indoor riding school. From the earliest days until the end a large majority of girls rode, many to a very high standard.

The founders set great stress on the spiritual development of the girls and this continued for the school's duration, with the Chaplain being also Priest-in-Charge of the parish and the school paying the greater part of his salary. The girls attended services in the parish church and were a distinctive sight walking through the village in their Harris tweed Sunday cloaks.

The number of students never exceeded 300 and the school was probably most comfortable at around 200, when each girl was known and was special. As boarding became concentrated on the two main sites Manor Farm, which had been a staff residence, became the Head's house, until Little Croft was built in 1985 on the site of Pop's garden, or the Italian Garden.

Until the last few years the "crocs", or crocodiles, through the village were a distinctive feature of the school as the girls walked up and down the A357 from Grange to Croft for gym, swimming, boarding, prep or meals. The reflective trips on their weekday navy cloaks caught many a motorist by surprise as he saw in the gathering gloom what appeared to be a large undulating caterpillar moving along the pavement.

Croft girls in their boaters, in 1987.

Manners and correct behaviour were rigorously maintained and long after most people had stopped wearing hats speechday at Croft saw a selection of headgear among the sixth-formers that would have put to shame a Buckingham Palace garden party. The younger pupils sported boaters and white gloves in the summer. How they grumbled, but what a furore there was when staff suggested boaters should be dropped from the uniform list.

Development continued. In 1986 new looseboxes, field shelters and a tackroom were added, named in memory of Headmistress Barbara Warley, allowing the old stables to be converted into further boarding accommodation. A sports hall and theatre were built on the Grange site in 1988 and opened by actor Anthony Andrews.

Upper sixth Croft House students on Speech Day 1993.

In 1993 weatherman Ian McCaskill opened a new science and classroom block. But the tide was beginning to turn. Girls' boarding was no longer as popular, the economic climate was less favourable and more boys schools were taking girls to ensure their own survival. Larger, more prestigious girls schools fought more keenly to keep their numbers up and, finally, what made Croft so special, its smallness, became its downfall. It had filled a very real need in the world of education, providing a personal environment where the girl who was not a confident, academic high-flyer could achieve without pressure. The results had been amazing. Many did go on to university but many who might have sunk without trace in mainstream schooling achieved highly and flourished in the gentle, caring environment of Croft House School.

After it closed, what had been Croft was converted into the Old School House and the attached dormitory block was demolished. The houses in Oak Court were built on the site of the old gym and swimming pool. Manor Farm and Little Croft became private houses. The Forum School took over the Grange site. In the parish church is a memorial to Caesar and Pop, and stained glass from the school chapel windows has been incorporated into the church windows. And thousands of Croft girls all over the world remained as living proof of the quality of education and training for life that the school gave.

To quote from Mrs Torkington's Review of the First Ten Years: "This is the life of Croft House. But what lies behind it? Our aims have failed if Croft is only just 'another school.' Our purpose is the development of character, our foundation a strong belief that Christian ideals are workable and that our primary duty is to learn to live together in this community as a family… The results? No one can ever tell. The future alone will show the result of our work and thought here."

A Teacher's Memories

*Biology teacher Joan Venn recalls what happened when she went for
an interview at Croft on 2nd November 1966:*

"I was shown to Mrs Torkington's drawing room on the first floor, a lovely room
with an almost circular window. There we were, Mrs Torkington in an armchair,
her boxer dog and me on the settee. It seemed to be the dog's idea to push me off
the settee and I resisted this. I wondered later if this was the crucial test – if the
candidate resisted she was deemed assertive enough to teach.

"I don't remember much of the interview but shortly the bursar came in. 'Has
Miss Venn accepted?' she asked. I hadn't noticed being offered the job but, 'Oh
yes, I think so,' said Mrs T and the bursar withdrew and came back with a form
which I duly signed.

"The advertisement for my job, a new one in the school, was the result of two
sisters saying they would like to go to Oxford to do zoology. 'Oh, we'll get
someone,' said Casear, as she was known to all, and called to her face. The
imperial aura fitted well. She was a tall, commanding figure who could appear
forbidding but was in fact most kind, even indulgent to the girls.

"We single staff were farmed out in the village to hostesses who were not
overpaid for giving us a bed and a weekly bath. We had all our meals at Manor
Farm. The cook was Mrs Savory and she fed us like fighting cocks. The Manor
was in fact our 'officers mess' only it was always so cold in winter, we didn't care
for it much.

"The form rooms at Grange were little more than wooden sheds but the chemistry
and biology labs were better and separate from the other rooms. Mrs Torkington
lived at Croft but drove down each morning, with the dog, to take assembly which
she did splendidly with dignity and authority. She then briefly reviewed her
empire and departed to Croft only occasionally to return to teach some Scripture.

"She and an assistant, Mrs McKillop, were brilliant at entertaining prospective
parents. Mrs T always made the visitors feel really welcome and assumed they
had already accepted. I'm sure they generally had if she approved of them.

"Throughout my 13 years at the school I remember the very happy, interesting
group of people who were the teaching staff. If there was any little local difficulty,
the person to consult was Percy Butt, the head gardener. One speechday rehearsal
was a case in point. Mrs Torkington could not abide mini-skirts and although
school skirts were a regulation length, mysteriously what was worn was always
quite a bit shorter. When we rehearsed the girls receiving their prizes, their
accustomed bob on quite a high platform did show that this was not a suitable
performance. 'Do something about it,' I was told, so I went to Percy. He added a
standard fuchsia to the plants at the front of the platform. It was perfect and
speechday was the splendid day it always was, a real gala for all the village.

"Retirement was not something that appealed to Mrs Torkington but when she
was 72 the governors made it happen… The new Head was a disaster, an

unsuitable person who reigned for five terms before she was asked to leave. She decided A-level classes would be taught with Clayesmore, at that school, and the chemist and I were sacked. We went to Uplands School in Parkstone but I was invited back to Croft when the Warleys (Barbara and Eric) rescued the school…"

FOOTNOTE: *"The sisters for whom I had been recruited went to Oxford and did very well, and I am still in Shillingstone – one of only a few survivors. I am sorry that Croft House School does not add to life in Shillingstone any more."*

Above: The Portman Hall in 2000 - still serving its community 44 years on, but, with parking problems and hefty repair bills, now in need of replacement.

Below: The Reading Room which started its life as the Church Room, became home to Shillingstone Youth Club in the last quarter of the 20th century and has now been converted into a private house.

Chapter 9

Leisure Time

Long gone are the days of a weekly market granted to Bryan-de-Turbervill, Lord of the Okeford Skelin Manor in the time of Edward III, together with the right to celebrate the feasts of St Barnabas and St Denis. The former, held on 9th June gave rise to Shillingstone's traditional annual fête. This became a holiday, now lost, and took the form of a street fair with a procession, numerous sideshows and dancing round the maypole on the then larger village green. Tea and more dancing followed on the parson's lawn, before retiring to the Ox Inn where further celebration continued into the night. The Rev Cooke speaks of old Vanner, a fiddler from Fifehead Neville, who provided the music given sufficient encouragement.

The maypole brought Shillingstone some fame as it was boasted to be 110 feet 1 inch in height, with another 8 feet 5 inches in the ground, inspiring William Barnes to poetry:

Dancing round the maypole in the early 1920s.

> "And Shillingstone, that on her height
> Shows up her tower to op'ning day,
> And high-shot Maypole yearly dight
> With flowry wreaths of merry May."

The pole was blown down in 1890 but renewed in 1903 and maintained until 1939 when it was finally taken down just before World War II.

A traditional mummers play survived up until the 1890s, being described by the Rev Cooke as "formal, undramatic and incredibly dull." However, the Shillingstone Bull or Ooser, linked to these festivities, must have livened things up. He rampaged the village dressed in a bull's hide with a huge horned mask adorned with hair, beard and a hinged jaw. A mediaeval fertility symbol, he made the round of the houses in a wild, uncontrolled fashion, frightening all and threatening the women, until rewarded with refreshment.

More recently, village fêtes took place

Mike Dove, who helped to revive the annual sports festival, masterminds the 1998 event on the recreation ground...

... while Paul Moore and Brian Crabb take care of the skittles contest.

on the recreation field, a sports ground given to the village by Sir George Lowndes in 1927. This provided a venue for a thriving cricket team and for an annual sports festival, which has been resurrected recently. The pavilion was paid for by public subscription in 1934 and a grass tennis court, later replaced by two all-weather courts, was donated by Mrs Portman.

Originally the June fête was a combined village effort with the usual activities including a street procession, fancy dress and the crowning of the Rose Queen, a girl from the village. On many occasions Shillingstone House became the preferred venue, largely because of the centrepiece provided by Sir Thomas Sal 's light railway.

Carol singing, possibly a less exciting but well-supported event, took place with the help of Reg Sloper's lorry so that outlying parts of the village could be reached. Singing was more of a family and community pastime then and the village had an excellent male voice choir, mainly made up of railway personnel. They performed in the Village Hut, a building that holds fond memories for some older villagers.

Transport being limited to two or four legs, entertainment was largely within the community. As little as 60 years ago it was difficult for an outsider to court a girl from the village. We grumble about the traffic, but it has helped in that respect.

Church Room – Village Hut – Portman Hall

THE Church Room or Reading Room was built and furnished by Mrs Kyrle Chapman in 1895 on land given by Viscount Portman at a nominal rent. The building was given for the benefit of the village and was originally used for church meetings, the Band of Hope, the Communicants Guild and for educational classes. They retained this Victorian didactic intention until after World War I, when the building was used almost exclusively by the Working Men's Club.

The Village Hut, a World War I Army Hut, was given to the village by Mrs Webber in 1926 with a somewhat different aim. The war was over and the 1930s slump was yet to come. The Hut became a thriving social centre reflecting the nation's determination to enjoy itself. Functions included concerts, magic-lantern shows, children's Christmas parties, dances and whist drives, and it was a meeting place for Guides and Brownies, Mothers Union, Women's Institute – who paid "the small charge of 1s" for their monthly meetings – and, later, the Home Guard. The library had free use of it on Friday afternoons, and the Jam Centre was allowed the use of the youth club cupboard during the jam-making season.

At the outbreak of World War II in 1939 the Hut was requisitioned for billeting purposes, for which the Shillingstone Social Committee which ran it received £39. By 1941 the building had been returned to the village. A farewell dance was arranged for the departing Northumberland Fusiliers and in February a tea was given for 230 members of His Majesty's armed forces who had paraded for Warship Week. Links to the war effort continued. Dances were held to raise money for gasmasks, and donations from the Hut proceeds were also sent

Guides of the 1940s... From left: Sheila (or Isabel) Aimee, Irene Potasnic, Pamela Brown, Beryl Baker, Jean Pope, Pamela Read, Grace Symes and Pam Snook.

Brownies of the 1980s... From left: Lorraine Ellis, Sophie Lamper, Demelza Watts, Joanna Lloyd-Jones, Alison Fry, Joanna Tew, Victoria Sanders and Emma Cross. Picture by John Lamper.

regularly to the Deep Sea Fishermen and Minesweepers Wool Fund, the Red Cross Prisoner-of-War Fund, the Empire Air Raid Distress Fund, the Empire Cancer Campaign and Shillingstone's own first-aid point. During 1942, the minute book reveals, a total of £100 9s 9d was paid out "to various deserving causes."

Dances in the Hut were especially popular, often being held twice a week in those pre-telly times. At one held during the summer of 1942 the social committee agreed that any members of the Sussex Yeomanry who came should be allowed in free of charge. And later that year there was another farewell dance, this time for "the boys of the 166th Newfoundland Regiment."

Shillingstone's own "local boys and girls" serving elsewhere with H M forces were not forgotten by the committee either – they were all sent 5s savings stamps on greetings cards as Christmas presents.

During the early 1950s, records and correspondence suggest a decline in use and interest, together with some deterioration in the building itself. It was then that mention was first made of a possible new village hall to be built on the same site. At the same time efforts were made by the Hut committee and the parish council to buy back the Church Rooms and the Hut from the diocese, which was achieved in due course.

In 1956 the foundation stone was laid for the £8,000 new hall, most of the funding for which came from Mrs Florence Portman. By July 1957 the inaugural meeting of the Portman Hall Committee was held, and the official opening by Mrs Portman on Saturday 14th September 1957 was extensively reported in *The Western Gazette* the following Friday, 20th September. It was described as "one of the best-equipped halls of its kind in Dorset." A special dance on the evening of the official opening, with music from the Dixielanders Band, was MC'd by Mike Dove. From the outset the hall committee included representatives from the parochial church council, the parish council, Scouts and Guides, the village school PTA, the men's club, the tennis club, the British Legion, the Conservative

Club, the WI and the cricket club.

As time went on, other organisations made use of the building, and it was also increasingly used by people from outside the village for weddings and parties. The hall now resounds to the activities of the playgroup, the thump of keep-fit music, the quieter tones of the Seniors Club, the singing call of line dancing and the rhyming shouts of the bingo caller. Shamdram and Babysham entertain audiences there, and the professional theatre visits from time to time under the guidance of Artsreach. Spring fairs, harvest suppers and Christmas parties punctuate the years. Whist drives, jumble sales and parish council meetings are other regular activities...

The Portman Hall is in almost constant use – it had 394 bookings on 245 days in 1999 – and over the years the facilities have steadily improved. But the problem of parking, never foreseen in 1956, has yet to be overcome. That is one of the main reasons, along with the need for some £60,000 worth of repair and maintenance work, why at the beginning of the 21st century, 44 years on, a village amenities committee was set up by the parish council to look into the feasibility of starting all over again with another brand new village hall somewhere else in Shillingstone.

Lady Portman lays the foundation stone of the Portman Hall in October 1956.

The Skyliners

FRED Savory's musical memories of Shillingstone in the 1950s include the skiffle group he set up with his two younger brothers, Raymond and Alan, and his friends Reg Crane, Nigel Starks, Roy Scammell, Derek Snook, Rodney Galpin and Dave Rose.

"All of us had guitars," he said, "but none of us could play a note." The group used to sit on a bench down on the recreation ground and strum away "making all the ungodly and unearthly noises that ever any man could hear." Then one day Fred decided to buy a book on simple guitar notes. With the aid of that plus an old washboard they acquired, and a tea-chest and broom for the bass, the

*The Shillingstone
Skyliners in the
1950s, with guitars
and washboard.*

Skyliners, as they decided to call themselves, were born. All of them could sing too, and some of them learned to harmonise.

The parish council allowed them to use the pavilion on the rec as a practice room and, hesitantly, they made their debut at a dance in the Portman Hall, putting on a turn in the interval to give Roy Kay on his Hammond organ a break. Next came a party in the hall which the village school PTA was organising. "That went really well," said Fred, "and after it we were away."

For the couple of years they were in existence the Skyliners were in demand not just at village hops but at fêtes in other nearby villages, at Blandford Camp, a the Tithe Barn in Hinton St Mary, even at the Arcade Ballroom in Boscombe. Sadly, though, they never cut a disc and there are no sound archives of their music.

The Cricket Club

SHILLINGSTONE Cricket Club was formed in 1910, at first playing friendly matches on Saturdays and in the evenings. Sunday cricket was first played in 1951 and flourishes today. Throughout the whole history of the club it has received strong support from within the village, not just in terms of players but also in keeping one of the most immaculate grounds in Dorset and the providing of cricket teas unsurpassed anywhere.

There have been many wonderful days of cricket at Shillingstone recreation ground. One of the most successful years was 1972 when the club entered the National Haig Village Cricket Competition (well remembered for the bottle of Haig whisky each club received every round of the competition and, in

Shillingstone's case, always exchanged at the Old Ox for beer). A total of 795 clubs entered from all over the country and Shillingstone became the Dorset group winner after a series of exciting matches including a one-wicket win over Milton Abbas and a win over top league club Beaminster in the semi-final when Shillingstone, batting first, scored exactly 100, only to bowl their opponents out for 99. In the final, Shillingstone made 152 for 2 against Wimborne St Giles, and ran out winners by 13 runs.

In the next round Shillingstone travelled in two coaches to play Shrivenham, and on a damp pitch scored 139 for 7. The Wiltshire champions had no answer to the power of Shillingstone's bowling and could only reach 100.

With dreams of a day at Lords, Shillingstone entertained Cornish champions Troon in the next round in front of the largest cricket crowd ever seen on the recreation ground (over 200 cars and seven coaches) but it was not to be, and Troon won by nine wickets. However, Shillingstone did send a coachload of players and supporters to the national final at Lords to see Troon become the overall winners. Though never again reaching the 1972 heights, Shillingstone did win the Dorset section again in 1974 and were runners-up in 1982.

Shillingstone started playing league cricket in 1973, eventually winning the Dorset junior championship in 1980. This ushered in a very successful period with similar successes in 1981 and 1983, and finishing runners-up in 1985. The league was reorganised in 1986 with Shillingstone in division one for several years. As the players of the 1970s and 1980s got a bit older the standard dropped, as did Shillingstone's league position, but in 1996 those leaner years were ended by the winning of the Dorset (Sunday) league division three, losing only one match all season. Shillingstone currently plays successfully in division two with a mixture of young and older players. The club also plays regular evening cricket in the Fanston league, winning the knockout cup in 1983, and the division two title in 1988, 1995 and 1997.

The Shillingstone cricket team that was the Dorset group winner in the 1972 National Haig Village Cricket Competition and came close to the finals at Lords. Back row from left: Pete Hawkins, Roy Paulley (scorer), Gordon Wells, Pat Crane, Gerry "Petal" Ridout, Dave Mace, Edgar Sheen. Front row: Terry Hawkins, Alan Hunt, Derek Crane (captain), Norman Hardy (vice-captain), Graham Hawkins.

Going places (above)... A Band of Hope outing to Weymouth in 1924 – note the vehicle's 12mph speed limit... And a WI outing in a similar charabanc from Bird Bros of Yeovil

Summer fun days (right) in the river in the 1920s.

And (below) entering into the spirit of the Coronation celebrations of Queen Elizabeth II in 1953, Shillingstone's fancy dress parade heads out from Church Road.

Footballers in Shillingstone have come and gone but there was strong support for this game in, for example, the early 1950s and the late 80s.

The squad of 1952-53 included, back row from left: Fred Light, Ted Hallett, Bill Woolridge, Jim Stone, Les Jackson, Johnny Price, Ernie Ricketts, Jim Rawles, Bert Laws, George Galpin. Front row: E R (Joe) Harvey, Ken Savory, Sid Fudge, Bill Bealing, Heinz Graeser.

And among those involved in 1988-89 were, back row from left: David Crane, Stephen Hawkins, Gary Crane, Simon Poole, Adrian Royal, Neil Hilyard, Glenn Davis, Alan Royal, Brian Crabb. Front row: Alistair Underwood, Julian Crane, Peter Purnell, Gary Hawkins, Alan Read, Steven Brine. Picture by Simon Hunt.

Shillingstone also hosts many county youth games (11-16 years), which is again a reflection of the high standard of preparation and care taken at the club. A young Shillingstone player, Chris Green, toured Canada with Dorset in 1991.

Over the years there have been a large number of people who have made great contributions to the club and, while it would be impossible to acknowledge all of them, special mention must go to Roy Paulley (whose son, Ian, in 1994 was the first batsman in the Dorset league to score 1,000 runs in one season) and to Dave Crane who maintains the club's ground so well – for may years on a tractor registered in April 1955 and bought by the cricket club in 1972 but replaced before the end of the century.

Every year since 1972 the club has held a dinner-dance with a large proportion of the players, supporters and helpers congregating to celebrate the past season and look forward to the next – especially the tea intervals.

The King's Shilling

A village experience, linking the present with the past, is recalled by one of those involved...

ONCE in a while a community comes together to share an experience that is recorded and remembered for ever. One such occasion was the tragedy of the First World War, when Shillingstone was bled of its young men. But this sad event became the main theme in a happy and memorable event in 1987 when John Oram and the Colway Trust agreed to produce a Shillingstone Community Play.

Writing and producing the play took a year. Three professional drama specialists came to live in the village, to be part of the community. These good people were to be our guides, teachers and friends. A team of researchers scoured the county library and archives. In spite of being greeted with the comment: "Did anything happen in Shillingstone?" they uncovered much, although a lot came from the memories of the older residents.

Selecting the turn of the century and the years that followed, John Oram delivered an imaginative and evocative play that developed into a spectacular 10-night production. It was called The King's Shilling. Some 60 people took part, chiefly villagers. Croft House School joined in and gave us the use of their new drama studio. We raised funds, made costumes, masks and outrageous animals, learnt to sing, rehearsed, drank beer and partied together, raised more funds and rehearsed some more.

To mark the event the village maypole was resurrected. A 90-year-old Redwood cedar, given by Sir Michael Salt, was felled, stripped of its bark, transported to the recreation ground on a lorry from Antell's Garage to be finally, and with several anxious moments, erected on the playing field. Not quite the 110 feet of the original, it stands an impressive 65 feet tall and is capped by a gold-painted wooden finial turned by Graham Collier.

On 24th November1987 the clock rang the changes of a new century with the opening performance of The King's Shilling. The parade of time carried the promenading audiences with it through the extraordinary happenings of an ordinary village – a runaway pig, a flying fish, a nightmare of frogs, a marriage, a birth, a death. The castle cat and the Ooser appeared in the village again. Families came to life – Snooks, Fudges, Coles, Trowbridges, Beaumonts, Browns and Toozes. Then the war, and the bravery and sorrow of it all. We learnt to love the nostalgic songs which finally on the Saturday, our last night, brought us all to tears. But the real end was the ritual burning of all the props and effects, then a happy party with its sad partings.

Those who were involved grew closer to each other and to their village through their new knowledge of what had gone before.

Enter Artsreach

Professional drama arrived in rural communities in the last years of the 20th century thanks to an initiative called Artsreach. Through this, small and enthusiastic touring companies take their often amazingly ambitious shows around a number of village halls and, thanks to retired teacher Mike Dove, Shillingstone is on their regular itinerary. One such group is Hijinx Theatre, and Mr Dove describes a typical working day for them...

HIJINX Theatre's loaded van left Cardiff around midday, arriving at the Portman Hall at 3.30pm. A little later an overloaded and somewhat tired Ford Fiesta followed. When strewn across the hall floor, the contents of the van looked to be enough to fill three such vehicles. At 5pm it was tea and buns all round and then by 6.30pm the cast were warming up to strange mouth music which resembled those haunting recordings of whale talk.

With lights lowered and the stage set, people drift in. Five minutes to go. House lights go out, spots illuminate the stage and quite suddenly the world closes to a 15ft square in the centre of the room. Noisy traffic outside goes unnoticed, the village and the world retreat. Concentration is total but effortless. Quickly players become persons and persons characters – as relationships develop, each becomes exposed. The black and white fragments become a coloured whole as the jigsaw slots together. The technician works his magic with his box of techno-tricks, weaving a convincing reality. Conviction brings empathy as we explore their passions, wonder at their subtlety, their complexity of character and through it all discover ourselves.

Quite suddenly the play is finished. We wait, momentarily suspended, then thoughtful applause grows with enthusiasm. The lights lift, the clapping eases and stops. Some turn to go, some share the still-fresh experience, exchange greetings, congratulate the cast, then leave.

The women's comic football team that took the field in 1942. They may have aged a tiny bit, but the names are still familiar. From left: Mrs Nellie Hart, Mrs May Hooper, Mrs Eve Laws, Mrs Mary Conduit, Mrs Elkins, Mrs Ada Rampton, Mrs Christine Pope, Mrs Evelyn Munday, Mrs Lucy Hallett, Mrs Ruth Trowbridge, Mrs Hilda Warren, Mrs Phyllis Lane, Mrs Betty Savory.

And the men's comic team of the same vintage included (from left) Tuffin, Stone, Laws, Hooper, Savory, Sloper, Gregory, anon, Starkes, Robins, Hart, Oliver.

Shillingstone's male voice choir of the 1930s, cup winners in the Dorset Choral Competitions. Back row from left: Charlie Butt, George Laws, Ron Sloper, Reg Sloper, Billie Brown, Col Torkington, Joe White, H Tate, W Lanning, Dan Hunt. Front row: Dan Ridout, George Cole (conductor), Alan Moore, Harold Hooper, Douglas Rogers.

With easy banter, still high on adrenaline, the players collapse the set, feeding it neatly into the waiting van. Doors slam, they pull away. It's 11pm. Wondering what each receives for their 11-hour day, I turn the key and misquoting the Bard murmur: "The stage is all the world."

A village school pageant at Broadclose.

Taking a break from haymaking during World War II – Mrs Phyllis Lane with daughter Sylvia (right) and two evacuees from Kennington who came to stay with them to escape from the blitz.

143

ANNEX

Roll of honour

The list of all the men from Shillingstone who served in H M Forces in World War I

Lieut-Colonel H H Tasker, 1st City of London Regiment
Commander Charles Forbes
Commander Wyndham Forbes, DSO, Croix de Guerre
Major Jack Forbes, RGA
Major Vivian H Seymer, DSO, MC, RFA
Major R I Tasker, 11th County of London Regiment, JP, TD
Captain Athol Chichester, Devons
Captain Charles Quarrel, Royal Sussex Regiment
Captain Charles Adams, Welsh Guards
Lieutenant Raymond Trent, MC, 8th Somerset Light Infantry
Lieutenant Charles J Quarrel, 8th Royal Berks
Lieutenant Richard F Lowndes, 60th Rifle Brigade

Name	Rank	Regiment
Albert E Adams	Gunner	RGA
Robert J Adams	Private	Canadian Mac Gun Corps
Victor Adams	Cadet	RAF
Robert J Ames	Sergt-Major	Dorset Territorials
William Ames	Private	Dorset Yeomanry
Charles Bartlett	Driver	RASC
Thomas Bastable	Private	4th Hussars
Albert Booth	Private	RAF
Charles Bown	Gunner	RGA
William Bown	Sergeant	Mt RASC
Fredk Bradley	Sergeant	Dorset Yeomanry
Jack Brown	Private	27th Canadian
Arthur C J Bushrod	Private	5th Dorsets
Fredk Bushrod	Private	Scottish Horse
George Butt	Private	Dorsets
Reginald Caines	Private	Coldstream Guards
Stafford C Candy	Private	Dorset Yeomanry
Arthur J Clarke	Private	County of London Yeomanry
John Clarke	Lance-Cpl	2nd Hants
William C Cox	Private	Dorsets
George Crane	Private	Dorsets
Regd Crane	Private	Dorsets
Robert Crane	Private	RFA
Cyril C A Curtis	Private	15th Hussars
Henry Curtis	Private	RFA
Ernest E Dance	Private	Dorsets
Charles Drew	Private	Dorsets
Reginald Eaton	Private	Coldstream Guards
Gilbert Forte	Private	RFA
William Freak	Private	Labour Batt
Edward J Gamage	Private	Dorsets
William Gatehouse	Private	Dorsets
Harry Gillan	Private	RAMC

Name	Rank	Regiment
Walter G Gillingham	Private	MG Corps
William Griffith	Private	RGA
Reginald Groves	Private	RFA
Harold Haines	Private	MG Corps
Percy Haines	Lance-Cpl	2nd Dorset
Ernest Hart	Private	Dorset Territorials,
Fredk Hart	Gunner	RGA
Regd S Hart	Private	RFA
Walter Hart	Private	RFA
Harry Hart	Driver	ASC
Jack Hart	Gunner	RMA, HMS *Good Hope*
Robert Hart	Private	2nd Dorsets
Philip Hart	Sergeant	Dorsets
Albert Hunt	Chief Boatman	Coastguards
Arthur Hunt	Sergeant	5th Somerset LI
Dan Hunt	Private	5th Royal Sussex
Harry Hopkinson	Private	RAMC
Bertram Inkpen	Private	Gordon Highlanders
Ernest J Inkpen	Sapper	Royal Engineers
Walter Inkpen	Sergeant	5th Dorsets
William Inkpen	Sergeant	5th Dorsets
Arthur G Jackson	Sapper	Royal Engineers
Fredk Jackson	Private	5th Dorsets
Walter Jackson	Private	Royal Engineers
Walter J Jackson	Sergeant	ASC
William Jackson	Private	2nd Hants
Ernest Jackson	Private	RGA
Albert Laws	Leadg Stoker	HMS *Queen Mary*
Fredk Laws	Private	Dorset Territorials
William J Laws	Gunner	RFA
Arthur Laws	Private	Wiltshire Regiment
George Laws	Private	Royal Berkshire Regiment
Harry Laws	Private	8th Hussars
William James Laws	Gunner	RFA
Albert Legg	Gunner	RGA
Douglas F Legg	Gunner	RGA
James Light	Private	1st Dorsets
Joseph Light	P O	RN, HMS *King George*
Harold Meaden	Private	6th Dorsets
James Meaden	Private	Dorsets
John Meaden	Private	Dorsets
Alfred Mesher	Private	ASC
Fredk J Moore	Gunner	RGA
John Moore	A B	Howe Batt, RND
Herbert Paulley	Private	Scots Guards
Edward S Philps	Private	1st Dorsets
William Poole	Gunner	RFA
William Pope	Private	2nd Dorsets
Fredk Pugh	Private	4th Dragoon Grds
Ernest Read	Private	1/5th Somerset Light Inf
Percy Read	Sergeant	6th Dorsets
Sidney Read	A B	Drake Batt, RND
A C Reed	Sergeant	2nd Hants
Regd C Reed	Private	Royal Berks Regt
Fred Ricketts	Gunner	RGA
Arthur F Ridout	Sergt-Major	9th City of London
Marwood A Ridout	Private	1/7 Hants
Percy O Ridout	Private	1/7 Devon Cyclists

Name	*Rank*	*Regiment*
William J Ridout	Private	1/7 Hants
Archie Robins	Sergt-Major	Royal Irish Regt
Percy Robins	Private	4th Hussars
Regd Robins	Sapper	Royal Engineers
David H Robins	Lance-Cpl	5th Dorsets
William J Robins	Private	RAMC
Alfred Rogers	Sapper	RCA Corps
Walter Rogers	Corporal	Royal Engineers
Richard S Roseveare	Private	Tank Corps
Walter Savory	Private	Somerset Light Inf
Wilfred Savory	Gunner	RFA
Archibald Score	Private	Dorsets
Reginald Score	Private	Dorsets
Regd Sibley	Driver	MT, ASC
Regd C P Simpson	Private	Dorsets
Albert Snook	Shoeing Smith	RFA
Jack Stainer	Corporal	2nd Hants
Tom Stainer	Private	2nd Scots Guards
William Stainer	1st Cl Stoker	RN
Bertram Starks	Private	RFA
Charles Starks	Private	Dorsets
George Starks	Private	ASC
Robert Starks	Private	RFA
Edward Starks	Corporal	1st Dorsets
Harry Starks	Private	RAF
James Starks	Sergt-Major	Royal Marines
William Starks	Private	DCLI
Walter Starks	Private	ASC
Charles Stone	Driver	ASC
Charles Stone	Private	Dorsets
Henry J Stone	Shoeing Smith	RFA
John E Stone	Gunner	RGA
Robert Stone	Wheeler	RND
Frank Suter	1st Cl P O	Coastguards
Ernest Tooze	Lance-Cpl	MGC Inf Brigade
Fred Tooze	Lance Cpl	2nd Dorsets
Regd Tooze	Corporal	6th Dragoon Guards
Frank Trowbridge	Private	RAMC
Jack Tucker	Private	16th Lancers
Regd Vine	Lance-Cpl	Royal Engineers
Harry Wareham	Seaman	RN, Torpedo Men
Ernest Webber	Private	Suffolks
Clement Witherby	Private	Australian Imp Force
Sidney White-Rogers	A B	Hawke Batt, RND
Charles Woolridge	Private	Labour Battalion
Ernest G Woolridge	Corporal	RFA
Herbert Woolridge	Private	5th Royal Sussex
Louis Woolridge	Private	Gloucesters
Jesse Woolridge	Private	Coldstream Guards

Village Trail

A walk around part of the village of Shillingstone will enable you to learn something of the history and development of the settlement over the centuries. It will probably be most convenient to begin the trail at the church…

As you walk along the footpath to the church, enjoy the panoramic views across the valley of the River Stour to Hambledon Hill, crowned by the massive earthen ramparts of the Iron Age fort, a settlement of more than 2,000 inhabitants longer than 2,000 years ago. On the skyline is silhouetted the 5,000-year-old long barrow, the tomb of chieftains of the Neolithic inhabitants of this area.

Holy Rood Church (1 on the map). There is an excellent guide on sale in the church (and a donation to church funds is always appreciated). The original church is traditionally believed to have been founded around 635 by St Birinus. The carved head over the door in the church porch may be of him. Much of the building you see today dates from Norman times. The tower was added around 1450. and the interior was extensively restored in the late 1800s.

William Barnes, the Dorset dialect poet wrote "and Shillingstone that on her height Shows up her tower to op'ning day…", and from the churchyard you can see what a prominent site the church enjoys, with views all around.

The early Saxon and medieval village probably grew around the church on this high land above the river, and remained here until the Black Death in the 14th century.

(Not included in the trail is the old **railway station**, the last surviving one on the Somerset and Dorset Railway closed in 1966. To reach it go through the kissing gate at the back of the churchyard, follow the footpath straight across the field to the stile, turn right and walk about 100 yards down to the station. From there is a pleasant walk south along the route of the old line bordering the River Stour.)

Walk back through the churchyard noting the base of the medieval preaching cross on the left, through the lychgate, a gift from Mrs Livingstone Learmouth in 1903, and back along the church path.

This is the centre of the old village, and the area bounded by **Church Road** was the village green, most of which was built on over the centuries. The open green was surrounded by several farms of which **Church House**, dating from 1710 (2), was one. On the other side of the lane is **Church Croft**, one of the few houses of squared stone in the village. It was built in the mid-1700s, and it was later the home of the estate carpenter and called Rose Cottage. Walk straight ahead, past the "new" rectory which is on the site of the old rectory barn and stables and the gardener's cottage. On the left is the coach house to the former rectory, now a comfortable home. Behind the high brick wall on the left is the **Old Rectory** (3) dating from the 1700s and much rebuilt in around 1890, now divided into two homes, one of which is the home of a noted daffodil breeder.

 Ahead is an attractive 18th century red brick thatched farmhouse, **Clayton Farm** (4), the last working farm of the many previously in the village. On the near right corner is **Croft Cottage** (5), a typical flint and brick cottage of the early 19th century. On the opposite right corner you will see the tall window of the former

Croft House (6). This was built in the late 19th century by Canon Dayman and from 1951 to 1995 housed Croft House School, a private girls school. It has now been converted back to private homes.

Walk over this "crossroads" into **Hine Town**, along the lane past several cottages for about 300 yards, and climb over the stile on the right. Follow the path across the paddock, one of the many open spaces in the village which make it so attractive. Cross another stile and follow the lane around to the main road. Opposite is **Cox House** (7), another thatched former farmhouse, its brick façade covering an earlier timbered structure perhaps dating back to the late 1500s. Turn left down the road and you shortly see the picturesque **Greensleeves** (8), one of the oldest houses in the village, built in the early 16th century, of timber frame, later refaced in brick at the front. It was probably single storey open to the roof with a central hearth. Part was a butcher's shop early in the 1900s. Opposite is the **Methodist Chapel** (9), built in 1904 and used for worship until 1995. All along this road were several more old thatched cottages which were demolished and replaced with modern houses and bungalows from the 1920s to the 1960s. Most of the land between the houses and all around the village was orchards. Virtually all have been destroyed in the past 100 years.

Continuing down the main road you pass **Stour House** (10), dating from 1760, though a new front was added in 1906. It was formerly the New Ox Inn until 1959, then The Good Earth tea shop, patronised by many famous personalities. At an earlier date it had also been the village undertakers.

Farther down the road is the Old Ox, still a thriving village pub, and opposite is **Cobbles** (11), a picturesque partly thatched house dating from the late 17th century, previously being tenements with the outbuilding being a malthouse. You now pass a number of attractive old thatched cottages and houses. **Hollies** (12) was partly built of cob in the mid-1700s and may have been a wheelwrights. Japonica Cottage is of stone and some cob, and Honeysuckle Cottage is of brick and cob. On the other side of the road are Wisteria Cottage, Lilac Cottage and Coombe Cottage, all mainly 18th century.

Cross the road with great care and walk up **Gunn Lane** past the Post Office. Take the first turning on the right and walk along **Everetts Lane**, a pleasant backwater. At Ivy Cottage where the surfaced road ends, continue ahead along the track which narrows to a footpath. On the left is a view of Shillingstone House, built in Victorian Gothic style in 1880. Turn left at the kissing gate. Over the wall on the right is **Manor House** (13) built in the 1920s to replace the Jacobean manor destroyed by fire. When you reach the main road turn left. On the opposite corner is another of the old thatched farmhouses which bordered the village green, 13th century **Manor Farmhouse** (14). The central core of the house may be even earlier. The **Victorian brick building** (15) between the filling station and the village shop was the Church Room and then the Reading Room, and lately the Youth Club. It has recently been converted into an attractive home. Opposite the shop is **Fippenny Cottage** (16), formerly Gaunts Farmhouse dating from the 17th century. The old building at the front of the bungalow next to the shop is the remaining part of the **village poorhouse** (17).

It is suggested you cross the main road here with great care, to the 18th century **Crooked House** (18), previously the first garage and motor repairer in the village. The old-style telephone box next to it is also a listed building dating from 1935! Just past here the road was much narrower as there was a thatched cottage built out into the road, demolished for road widening. On the other side of the road are

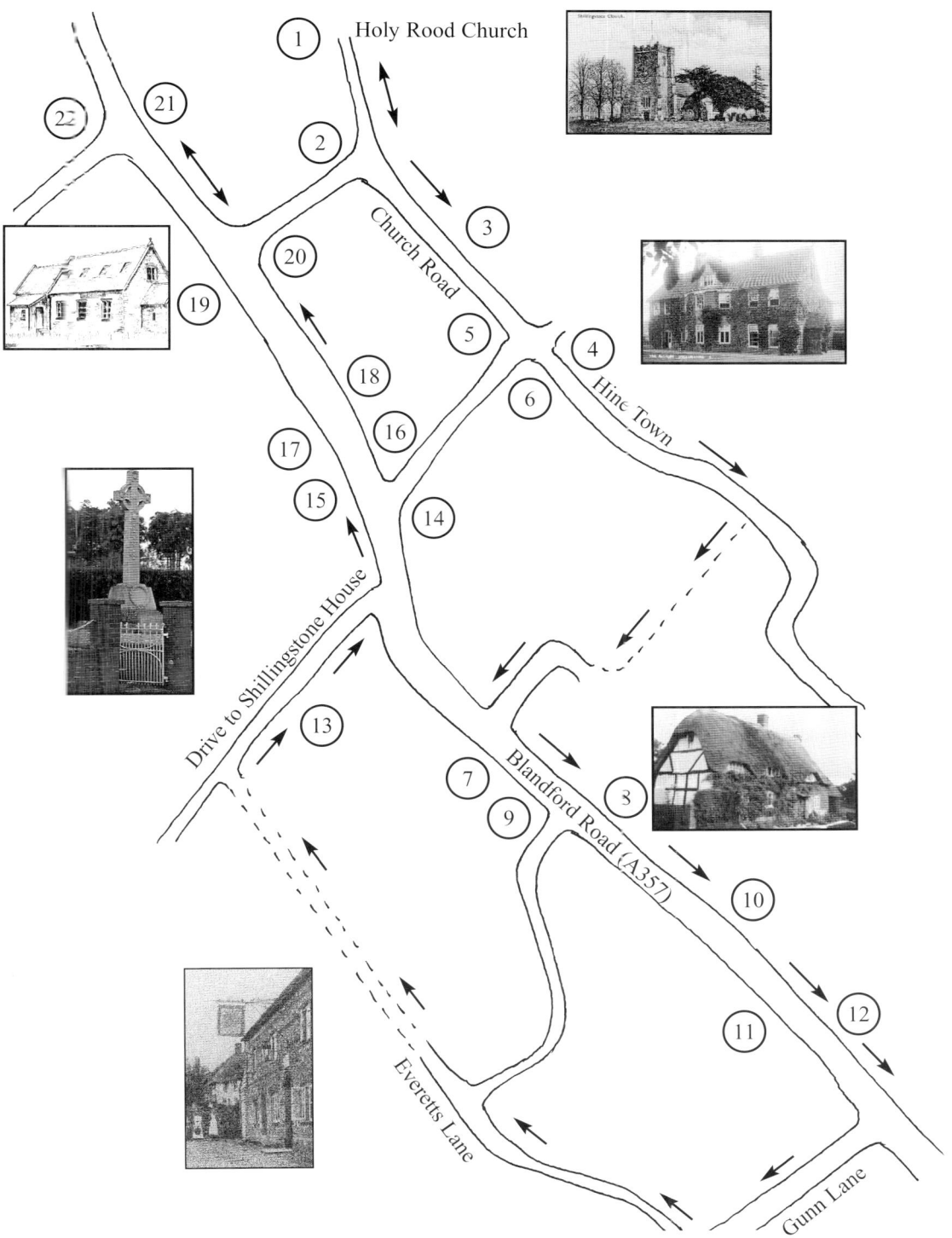

Holy Rood Church

1

21

22

2

Church Road

3

20

19

18

16

5

4

Hine Town

6

17

15

14

Drive to Shillingstone House

13

7

9

Blandford Road (A357)

3

10

11

12

Everetts Lane

Gunn Lane

two rows of cottages (19), nearly all thatched and dating mainly from the 18th century, though their core may be earlier still. Their front gardens were also victims of mid 20th century road widening. You can see that one of the houses once had a shop window. At the right hand end is Cross House, 17th century in origin, the left hand part of which is believed to have been a barn; note the old mullioned window in the end, now blocked up.

You now arrive at the **village cross** (20) and the surviving remnant of the village green, formerly the focus for village life when markets, fairs and festivities were held here. The steps and base of the cross have been dated to the 1400s but the shaft and cross head top were added in 1903 as a memorial to Mr Kyrle Chapman. The top is now badly eroded and is said to have been struck by lightning! Nearby stood the maypole at 110 feet in 1874, the tallest in Dorset if not in the whole of England. There was the following inscription on it:

> "The fading garland warns how short life's day,
> The towering May Pole heavenward points the way.
> Read thou the lesson – seek to gather now
> Undying wreaths to twine a deathless brow."

And William Barnes referred to it:

> "high-shot Maypole, yearly dight
> With flow'ry wreaths of Merry May."

Overlooking this tiny green is quaint thatched Maypole Cottage, built of brick and flint about 1750.

Continue along the main road past Tollbar Cottages, possibly replacing a toll house on the turnpike. The original post office was in this row of houses and the building opposite was the forge of the village blacksmith. Continue along to the **village school** (21) built in 1850, enlarged 1875, and since extended several times. On the side is mounted the old SHILLINGSTONE railway station sign. On the opposite side of the road is the **war memorial** (22), which commemorates the dead of two world wars, first dedicated on 24th September 1919. Alongside stood a captured German fieldgun, until this was donated to the war effort in the Second World War.

Retrace your steps back along the main road and turn left into **Church Road** to complete your walk.